Prehistoric Settlements of Eastern Thrace

A reconsideration

Burçin Erdoğu

BAR International Series 1424
2005

Published in 2016 by
BAR Publishing, Oxford

BAR International Series 1424

Prehistoric Settlements of Eastern Thrace

ISBN 9781841718637 paperback
ISBN 9781407328669 e-format
DOI https://doi.org/10.30861/9781841718637
A catalogue record for this book is available from the British Library

BAR Publishing is the trading name of British Archaeological Reports (Oxford) Ltd.
British Archaeological Reports was first incorporated in 1974 to publish the BAR
Series, International and British. In 1992 Hadrian Books Ltd became part of the BAR
group. This volume was originally published by Archaeopress in conjunction with
British Archaeological Reports (Oxford) Ltd / Hadrian Books Ltd, the Series
principal publisher, in 2005. This present volume is published by BAR Publishing,
2016.

BAR

PUBLISHING

BAR titles are available from:
       BAR Publishing
       122 Banbury Rd, Oxford, OX2 7BP, UK
EMAIL   info@barpublishing.com
PHONE +44 (0)1865 310431
  FAX   +44 (0)1865 316916
       www.barpublishing.com

CONTENTS

LIST OF FIGURES

PREFACE AND ACKNOWLEDGMENT

As the title indicates, this book is concerned with the prehistoric settlements of Eastern Thrace (Turkish Thrace). One of the problems in Turkish archaeology, with the exception of the University of Istanbul - Prehistory Section, was that the archaeological curriculum did not provide a place for the discussion of theory. Turkish archaeology, under the influence of the German archaeological tradition, is not founded upon innovative theoretical ideas but the documentation and collection of data. In this book an attempt has been made to break the traditional views.

The ideas presented here have been germinating since 1991. However, my vision of archaeology has changed since 1998, when I started a PhD at the University of Durham, and my interest began to focus on archaeological interpretation. I believe, to date, that there has been a lack of theoretical discussion as regards the archaeology of Eastern Thrace. This book is the product of intensive fieldwork undertaken in the Edirne region of Eastern Thrace, and it offers new information and theories on the prehistoric settlements of the region: it does not pretend to be a handbook on its prehistory. I think it is extremely important to evaluate some of the ideas proposed in this book by actually putting them into practice. I hope that this work will spark others to carry out the research needed to answer the questions about the archaeology of Eastern Thrace.

It seems evident that intensive archaeological surveys were only carried out across a small area of Eastern Thrace, and present excavations have still not revealed a complete picture of the cultural sequence of the region. I believe that more intensive surveys, large geomorphological investigations and more extensive excavations are needed.

Chapter I was published previously in *Proceedings of the Prehistoric Society* 2003. In this chapter, I discuss the extensive and intensive surface survey results in the Edirne region. This project concerned the settlement history of the region from the Neolithic to the Early Bronze Age. It includes systematic surveys for both off-site and site scatters, and intra-site gridded collection at selected sites. An earlier version of Chapter II appeared in *Documenta Praehistorica* 1999. This chapter concentrates on settlement mobility in the prehistoric settlements of Eastern Thrace as well as settlement types. I introduce two models for settlement mobility - extensive mobility and restricted mobility. In Chapter III, I discuss settlement territories in the prehistoric settlement of the Edirne region. For settlement pattern analysis of the Edirne region, I introduce a new model - the landscape model. An earlier version of Chapter IV has been published in *Documenta Praehistorica* 2000. In this chapter, I investigate prehistoric stone axe factories in Eastern Thrace, which are unique in the prehistoric record of the Balkans and Anatolia. The next chapter deals with explanatory models for the apparent dramatic decrease in population of Eastern Thrace in the Late Chalcolithic period. Another version of Chapter VI was previously published in the *European Journal of Archaeology* 2003. In this chapter, I suggest a different idea that is related to the symbolic value of landscape for island colonization.

I wish to express my deepest thanks to Dr. John Chapman and Prof. Anthony Harding of the University of Durham. Many of the ideas in this book have been developed through conversations with them. Special thanks are due to Dr. Ismail Fazlioğlu of the University of Thrace. Without his interest and help the intensive surface work would not have been possible. Thanks also to Alvaro Arce for his comments on an earlier draft of this book.

In 2001, I visited Romania for research. I should like to thank Prof. Dan Monah of the University of Iaşi, Prof. Dragomir Popovici of the National Museum of History in Bucharest and Dr. Gheorghe Dumitroaia of the Museum of Piatra Neamţ for their great hospitality and help. This visit was made possible by grants from the Prehistoric Society, the Graduate Society, and the Rosemary Cramp Fund.

I would like to extent my special thanks to all those who have helped in many ways, sometimes over many years. I have included their names in the list below. Any errors, omissions or misquotes etc., of course, remain entirely my own responsibility.

Dr. Işık Şahin, Prof. Alasdair Whittle, Güneş Duru, Prof. Nicolae Ursulescu, Prof. Mehmet Özdoğan, Prof. Hermann Parzinger, Prof. Ivan Gatsov, Lesley Harding, Prof. K. Leshtakov, Dr. Bisserka Gaydarska, Prof. Turan Efe, Prof. John Bintliff, Phill Howard, Mehmet Akif Işın, Valantin Radu, Moise Dragos, Prof. S. Marinescu-Bâlcu, Talat Dalaman, Dr. Miha Budja, Dr. Laurens Thissen, Dr. Onur Özbek, Nicola Dorian, Hanife Yalçın, Levent Çimen, Yavuz Babaçoğlu, Ahmet Aydın, Demet Uğraş, Dr. Mihriban Ozbasaran, The TAY Project, The Edirne Museum, The University of Durham-Department of Archaeology, The Graduate Society, The Prehistoric Society, The University of Thrace-Department of Archaeology, The Turkish Ministry of Culture.

Finally, to my parents (Aynur and Nevzat), I owe a debt that cannot adequately be expressed in words, and to them I dedicate this book. Very special thanks also go to Rabia Erdoğu for her support and help.

Some elements of my research were made possible by generous grants from the Prehistoric Society, the Graduate Society, University of Durham-Department of Archaeology, and a Birley Bursary Award.

PART I
BEYOND THE SETTLEMENTS

I-I OFF-SITE ARTEFACT DISTRIBUTION AND LAND USE

The analytical task of archaeology is to explain the density and character of the more or less focal but continuous distribution of artefacts. The high-density cores termed "sites" have traditionally been the focus of surveys. However, isolated artefacts and low density scatters have been recognised increasingly in recent years, and the term "non-site" or "off-site" started to be used (Dunnell and Dancey 1983; Thomas 1975; Foley 1981b; Bintliff and Snodgrass 1988 ; Bintliff; 2000). Since the mid 1970s, ethnoarchaeological studies focusing on the mobile or semi-sedentary subsistence-settlement systems of hunter-gatherer groups showed that much of the behaviour of hunter-gatherers creates discontinuous spreads of surface material over many hundreds of metres rather than discrete artefact clusters (e.g. Yellen 1977; Foley 1981a; 1981b). Archaeologists working in Britain, the Near East and the Mediterranean region discovered that off-site pottery scatters formed an almost unbroken carpet throughout the landscape and they considered that off-site archaeology is not only appropriate for studying mobile societies but also for more sedentary social groups.

For many different reasons, artefacts are discarded away from the settlements. Thus, off-site information is very significant for a comprehensive picture of land-use and clearly must be considered as one essential part of total survey design. Archaeological surveys concentrating on smaller study areas in Mediterranean, Britain and Near East, such as Boeotia (Bintliff and Snodgrass 1985; Bintliff 1992; Bintliff *et al.* 2000), Keos in Greece (Cherry *et al.* 1991), Kurban Höyük in Turkey (Wilkinson 1989), Hvar in Croatia (Gaffney *et al.* 1991), Nemea in Greece (Wright *et al.* 1990) and the Dalmatian coast of Croatia (Chapman *et al.* 1996), have provided important evidence relating to past land-use and settlement systems.

Up to now, there are no projects in Eastern Thrace or Western and North-western Turkey in which off-site materials have been recorded. One of the aims of our survey in the Edirne region of Eastern Thrace was to record off-site artefacts and to provide evidence relating to prehistoric land-use (Erdoğu 2002; 2003a).

Box A - The Land

Eastern Thrace (Turkish Thrace) acts as a land bridge between the Balkans and Anatolia. It is bordered on its west side by the Meriç (Maritsa, Evros) River, on its north and east side by the Istranca Mountain range, the Black Sea and Bosphorus, and on its south side by the Sea of Marmara and the Dardanelles (*Fig. A.1*). The undulating flatlands of the Ergene Basin constitute the main central plain of Eastern Thrace. The Ergene River rises far to the east as the Çorlu stream near Çerkezköy and flows westward across the centre of Eastern Thrace. It then skirts the foothills of the Southern highlands and joins the Meriç River. The confluence area of the Meriç and Ergene Rivers lies in a large flat basin, which today, is covered by marshes and rice fields. In prehistoric times a deep gulf existed in this basin (Göçmen 1976). The undulating flatlands of the Ergene basin constitute the main central plain of Eastern Thrace. The Ergene River receives numerous tributaries coming down from the Ganos Mountain, and also the Koru and Büyükhacı Mountains on the south. The largest stream called Ana, rises between the towns of Keşan and Malkara, and emerges north of the town of Hayrabolu, which gives its lower course its name. From the north, it receives a large number of streams coming from the Istranca Mountains, such as, Süloğlu, Akar, Koca, Şeytan, Poyralı, Ana and Sulucak (Admiralty Handbook 1917; 1942). The Ergene basin is densely cultivated, generally with wheat and sunflowers. However, heath, beet, sesame, corn and watermelon are also cultivated in various parts of the Ergene Basin.

The Tunca River is a tributary of the Meriç River, which rises in the Balkan Mountains, descends southwards, and joins the Meriç River below the town of Edirne. The width of the Tunca River is between 25 m and 40 m. During the dry periods of summer and autumn the river can be crossed by walk in many places (Admiralty Handbook 1917: 20).

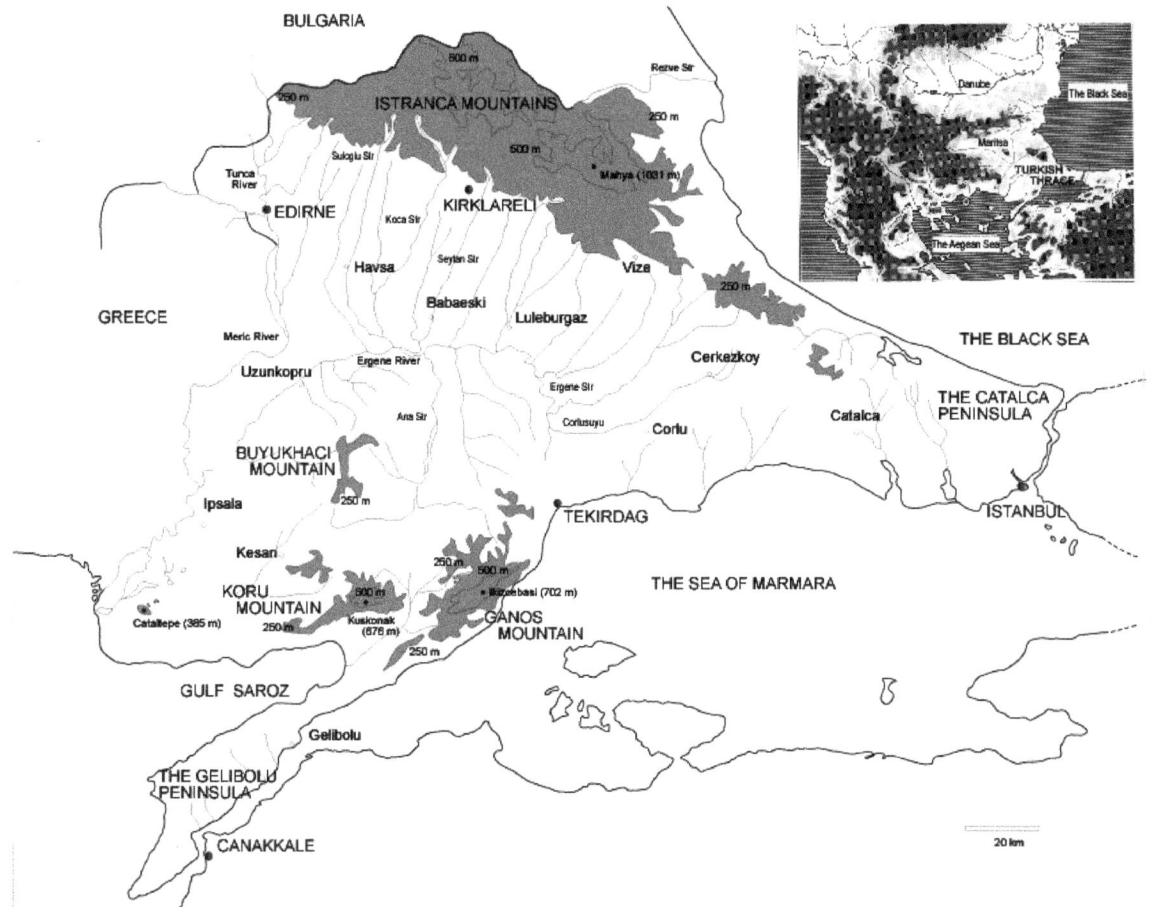

Fig. A.1. Map showing topographic features of Eastern Thrace (Turkish Thrace)

The Istranca Mountain range is the dominant physical feature of Eastern Thrace, which starts from the Çatalca area, continues parallel to the coast of the Black Sea and is connected to the Rhodope massive. Its peak, the Mahya, reaches a height of 1031 metres. On its south-western side, the Istranca Mountains consists of gentle slopes. On its north-eastern side, the ridge throws out an almost continuous series of spurs and hills close to the Black Sea (Admiralty Handbook 1917: 10).

The Black Sea coast of Eastern Thrace is generally exposed, dangerous and inaccessible. It is cliffed almost throughout its length, and fronted by rocks. The bay of İğneada is encumbered with rocks and reefs, and it is subject to sudden shifts of wind. The village of Kıyıköy (Midye) lies at the southend of Cape Seroz. It stands on the cliff between two valleys; Kazan and Papuç. From Kıyıköy almost to the end of the Çatalca promontory the smooth outline of the coast is unbroken save for the high rocky point of Cape Kastro and the broad cliffed headland of Cape Kara. Short streams from the northeast slopes of the Istranca Mountain range make insignificant breaks in the cliffs. Beyond the village of Podima the cliffs die out and the hills are lower until the Terkos stream. The Terkos Lake pounded back behind the high coast, and collects the water of several smaller valleys besides that of the Istranca Mountains (Admiralty Handbook 1942: 63). Behind the Çatalca line the country to the Bosphorus is plateau of fairly uniform heights. It is cut by valleys running parallel to each other from northwest to southeast. On the side of the

Sea of Marmara the coast is broken by river mouths, which form deep and safe estuaries (Admiralty Handbook 1917: 13; 1942: 120).

The Istranca Mountains contain important metal sources. Copper occurs in the Kırklareli region. There are important deposits in the areas of Dereköy, Şükrüpaşa and Armutveren on the Bulgarian border (Gültekin 1999; Wagner and Ozturnali 2000). There is some evidence for prehistoric mining in two locations – Ikiztepe and Dereköy (Wagner and Ozturnali 2000: 33). The Istranca Mountains are also potential sources for lead-copper (Ternek 1987). There are important iron deposits in the Kırklareli region, the area around Demirköy and Dereköy. Lalapaşa-Vaysal and Iğneada are potential areas for finding gold and silver deposits.

From Tekirdağ on the northern coast of the Sea of Marmara, the hills spread out westwards and northwards, forming a broken massive plateau. This plateau is the district of the Ganos, Koru and Büyükhacı Mountains. The Ganos Mountain is extending from northeast to southwest, steep towards the sea. Its highest point is İkizcebaşı with an elevation of about 702 metres. North-eastwards it is connected with the Ergene Plateau by low hills (Admiralty Handbook 1942: 118). The Koru Mountain is separated from the Ganos Mountain by the Kavak valley. Most of the surface is formed by steep-sided, flat-topped hills. Its highest point, Kuşkonak (365 m), lies north of the head of the Gulf Saroz. Westwards the Koru Mountain sinks into detected hills with the volcanic peak of Çataltepe (385 m) overlooking the town of Enez (Admiralty Handbook 1942: 118). Enez stands on the flat marshy delta-plain of Meriç, between the lakes of Dalyan and Gala. The Büyükhacı Mountain lies on the north of Koru Mountain. It consists of a thinly wooded plateau extending north-eastwards from the town of İpsala. It is enclosed by the angle of the Ergene-Meriç junction on the west, and by the headed-waters of the Ana Stream on the east. On the north it falls in easy slopes into the Ergene valley and on the south it falls over cultivated ground to the Büyük Stream (Admiralty Handbook 1917: 16).

The Gelibolu peninsula is also a part of Eastern Thrace. It is a very narrow and long piece of land, runs parallel to the Anatolian coast line, and is connected to the mainland of Thrace by an isthmus that is only 7 km in width (Admiralty Handbook 1917:17; 1942:71). The interior of the peninsula is a hilly country, cut up by streams. All the largest streams, except the Kocadere, drain to the Dardanelles. The eastern shores are formed by low cliffs. There are a number of well-protected harbours, such as Akbaş and Gelibolu. The western shores of the Gelibolu Peninsula are higher than the eastern side. It is steep and inaccessible, except for short beaches at the mouths of the few streams.

In Eastern Thrace, the climate is generally cool with moist winters and dry, hot summers. Certain climate differences can be observed in various parts. On the Black Sea coast the climate is sub-Mediterranean. The Edirne-Kirklareli region has a meso-Mediterranean, while in the Tekirdağ and Istanbul areas the climate is thermo-Mediterranean. There is a considerable temperature range, with January means below 2C° and July means above 25C°. Eastern Thrace is strongly influenced by winter depressions which pass frequently through the straits, but northerly winds of summer are much drier than along the Black Sea coast (Dewdney 1971). Consequently, total precipitation is much less, ranging from some 900 mm in the mountains to less than 600 mm in the Ergene Basin, and a larger proportion falls in the winter months. Summer rainfall occurs in short. June and August together have an average of only ten days with rain.

Surface Survey in Eastern Thrace

Our survey in Eastern Thrace, begun in 1995, was divided into two stages; extensive survey and intensive survey (Erdoğu 2002; 2003a). Extensive survey was conducted in small areas in the Edirne region to ensure coverage of as much altitudinal and environment variation as possible.

The method employed for the location of new sites was targeted fieldwalking in areas of supposed highest settlement density, with systematic collection of artefacts. This extensive survey gives a general idea of site densities and settlement patterns in the region. In 1995, the basins of Tunca, Süloğlu and the area along the southern fringes of the Istranca Mountains (see *Box A*) were investigated, while coverage was extended to the confluence area of the Meriç and Ergene Rivers in 1997 (*Fig. I.1*).

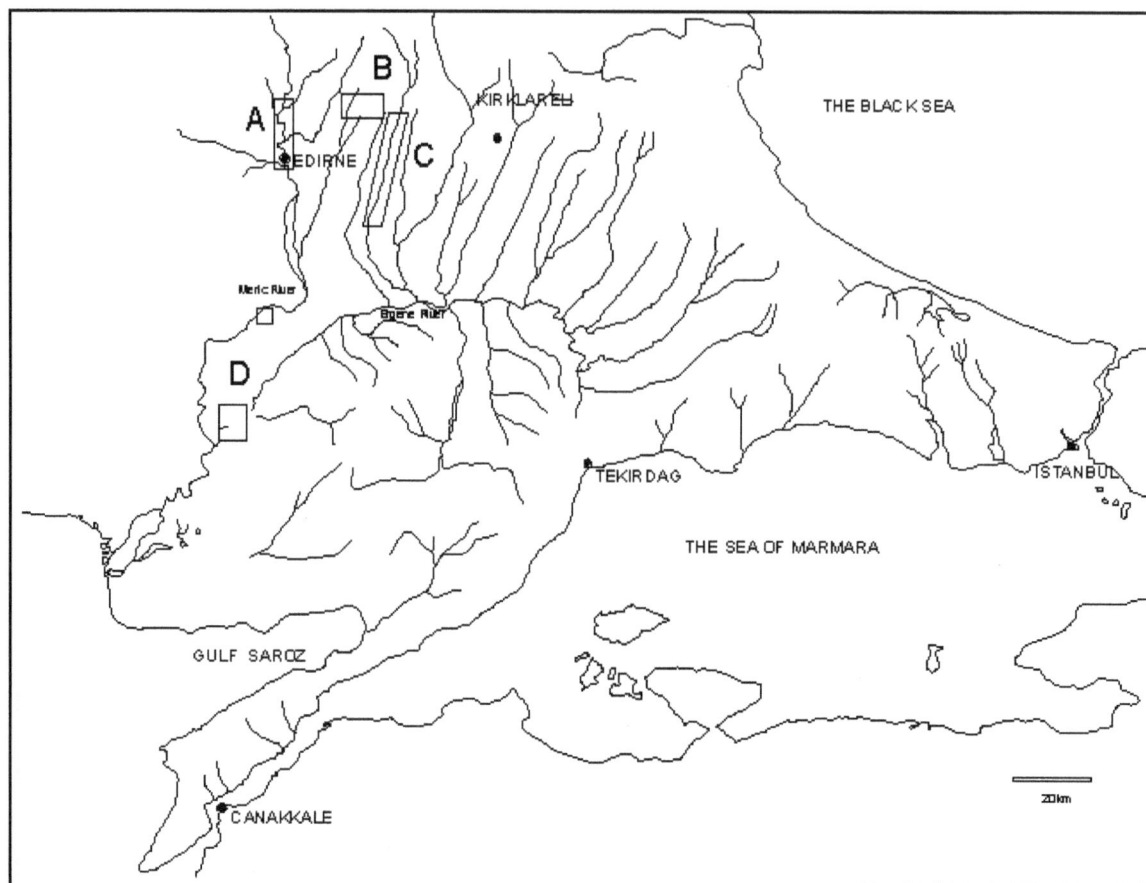

Fig. I.1. Location map of Survey Areas. A. The Tunca Basin. B. The area along the Southern fringes of the Istranca Mountains. C. The Süloğlu Basin. D. The confluence area of the Meriç and Ergene Rivers

The second stage was intensive survey, which involved two distinct procedures. The first off-site survey procedure was designed to investigate the outer perimeter of sites. Mapping off-site densities and comparing them with the presence, size and density of sites and the topography, promotes better understanding of the factors lying behind the formation of these remains and the more effective evaluation of their significance to the study of settlement patterns and land-use. Most of Eastern Thrace offered an important advantage for the adoption of an off-site approach. Almost the whole of the landscape is covered with agricultural fields a few meters wide. This clear subdivision of the whole survey area into a patch-work of individual small units offered a framework for the collection of off-site information. Each field unit was examined by a group of 4-5 people, walking in parallel lines spaced at 20 m or sometimes 10 m, depending on visibility. We accepted that each field walker has about 1 m front-visibility in each line. Thus every line was formed by 10 x 1 m "mini-transects" (*Fig. I.2*). A 100 x 100 m field unit was completed in ca. 10-12 minutes.

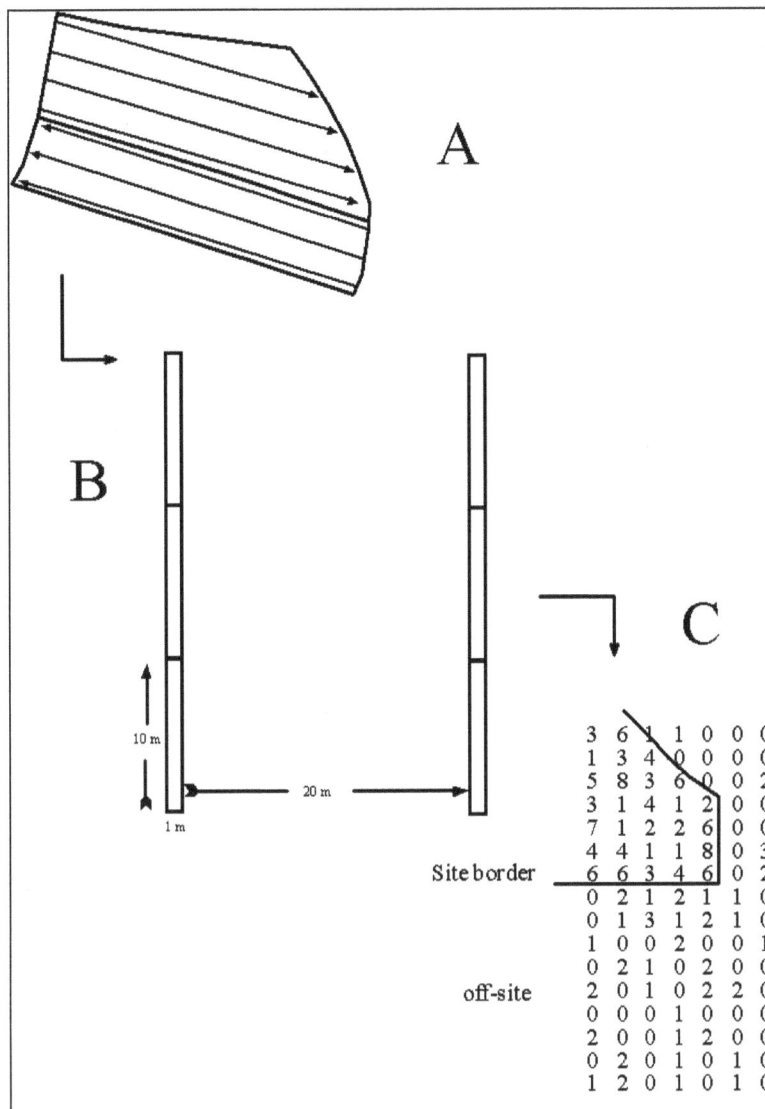

Fig. I.2. Schematic model of surface survey method in the Edirne region. A. Intra-site collection by transects in individual field units. B. Division of each field transect into 10 m - long mini-transects. C. Grid of pottery densities; each figure represents the number of sherds in a mini-transect. The site border is defined by a minimum of 6 sherds per mini-transect.

The second method involved the total collection of all surface artefacts within a 10x10 m. grid across the selected sites. These procedures show us the size and shape of the sites, and also artefact distributions in different periods. Artefacts collected from each squares were recorded on set forms under the heading of "sherd", "chipped stone" and other small finds, such as "figurine" or "stone axe".

Description of Extensive and Intensive Survey Areas

The Tunca basin: The Tunca River is a tributary of the Meriç River, which rises in the Balkan Mountains, descends southwards, and joins the Meriç River below the town of Edirne (see *Box A*). It forms numerous meanders. Geologically, Holocene alluvium covers the basement of the Tunca River. Continental Neocene deposits occur on both sides of the river (Ternek 1987). There is no detailed soil map of the area. According to a general (1;500,000) soil map, the flood-plain is covered by alluvial hydromorphic soils and the river terraces are covered by brown soils with rendzinas and grumsols (Dewdney 1971). The flat floodplain of the Tunca

River is flanked by low and high terraces. The terraces are now intensively cultivated with sunflowers and wheat. Göl Baba, west of the village of Büyük Döllük, is a former lake, which has been partially drained and now cultivated with rice.

The Tunca basin was partly investigated by the University of Istanbul in 1982 and 1986 (Özdoğan 1984: 66; 1988: 159). During our survey in 1995, six prehistoric sites were recorded (Erdoğu 1997: 274). No uplands and tributaries were investigated (*Fig. I.3*). During the Göl Baba pollen core fieldwork in 2002, two new prehistoric sites were also found around the former lake of Göl Baba.

The Süloğlu basin: The Süloğlu Stream is a tributary of the Ergene River, which rises near the village of Vaysal and runs from North to South (see *Box A*). The bed of the Süloğlu Stream is very narrow, but the area constitutes a very fertile plain ca. 1-1.5 km in width. The bed of the stream is covered by Holocene alluvium. Both side of the stream are flanked by low and high terraces that are suitable for settlement and agriculture. Geologically, the terraces are covered by undifferentiated continental Miocene and continental Pliocene deposits. The terraces are now intensively cultivated with sunflowers and wheat. There is no detailed soil map of the area. According to the general soil map, the flood-plain of the Süloğlu Stream is covered by alluvial hydromorphic soils whose the basic feature is poor drainage. Brown soils with rendzinas and grumsols occur on the terraces (Dewdney 1971).

The Süloğlu basin was first investigated by the University of Istanbul in 1982 (Özdoğan 1984: 66; 1985: 532). Our survey in 1995 was carried at by walking only stream terraces. Six prehistoric sites were recorded between the district centres of Havsa and Süloğlu (Erdoğu 1997: 278). With the exception of one site, most settlement is situated on the lower stream terraces, close to the stream (*Fig. I.4*).

The area along the southern fringes of the Istranca Mountains: The southern foothills of the Istranca Mountain are usually gentle and very fertile and rich in sources of water. The area is also close to copper and iron beds in the North. Geologically, the area consists of Marine Oligocene, middle Eocene and undifferentiated continental Miocene deposits. The marine Oligocene is differentiated into two units; the lower unit consists of marls and shales and the upper unit of lignite bearing sandstones. Again, there is no detailed soil map of the area; the general soil map shows most of the area to be covered, again, by brown soils with rendzinas and grumsols (Dewdney 1971).

Only a small part of the area was investigated in 1995 (Erdoğu 1997: 227). The survey was mainly carried out by walking based on information from the villagers. Five prehistoric settlements were recorded in the area. The settlements are concentrated along small streams or perennial tributaries, on natural lines of communication and generally close to water sources (*Fig. I.5*).

The confluence area of the Meriç and Ergene Rivers: The confluence of the Meriç and Ergene Rivers lies in a large flat basin, which today, is covered by marshes and rice fields. Holocene alluvium is well-developed in this area covering basements of the whole area. In prehistoric times, a deep gulf existed in this basin and during its recession, the basin was occupied by a lagoon and a series of shallow lakes, which were drained in the 1950s (Göçmen 1976). Andesites and andesitic tuffs also occur in this area and the tuffs are covered by Pliocene sandstones (Ercan 1992). Most of the area is covered by alluvial soils.

This basin and its North were chosen as the focus of the 1997 survey, because it was an unknown and important area. Recent alluviation hindered site visibility to a very high degree. Ten prehistoric settlements were recorded (Erdoğu 1999a).

Intensive block and transect surveys were conducted in two separate areas: 1. The Kavaklı-Ortakçı area, some 20 km northeast of the town of Edirne, along the Southern foothills of the Istranca Mountain; and 2. the Tepeyanı-Bağlariçi area, some 20 km east of Edirne in the Süloğlu Basin.

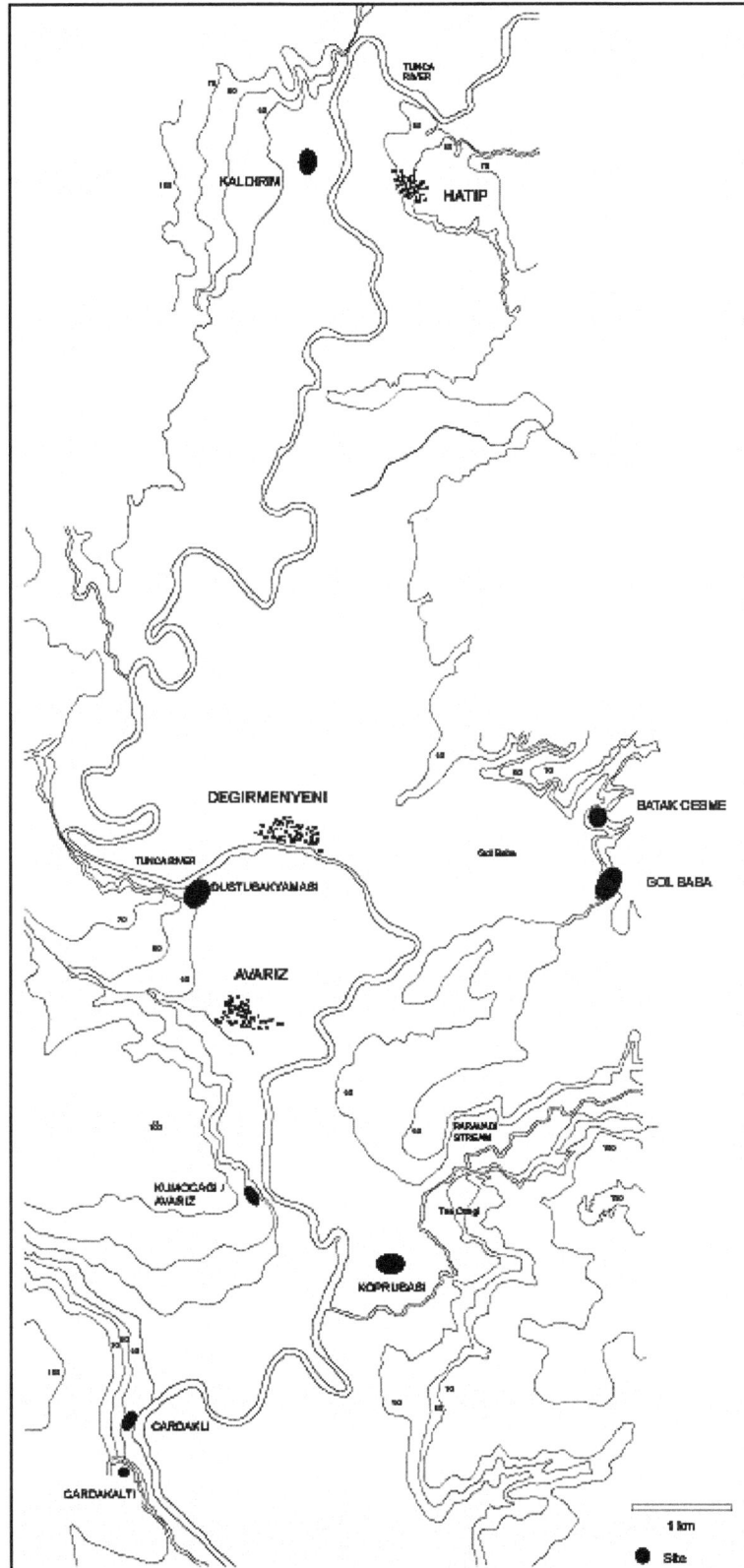

Fig. I.3. Distribution of Prehistoric settlements in the Tunca Basin

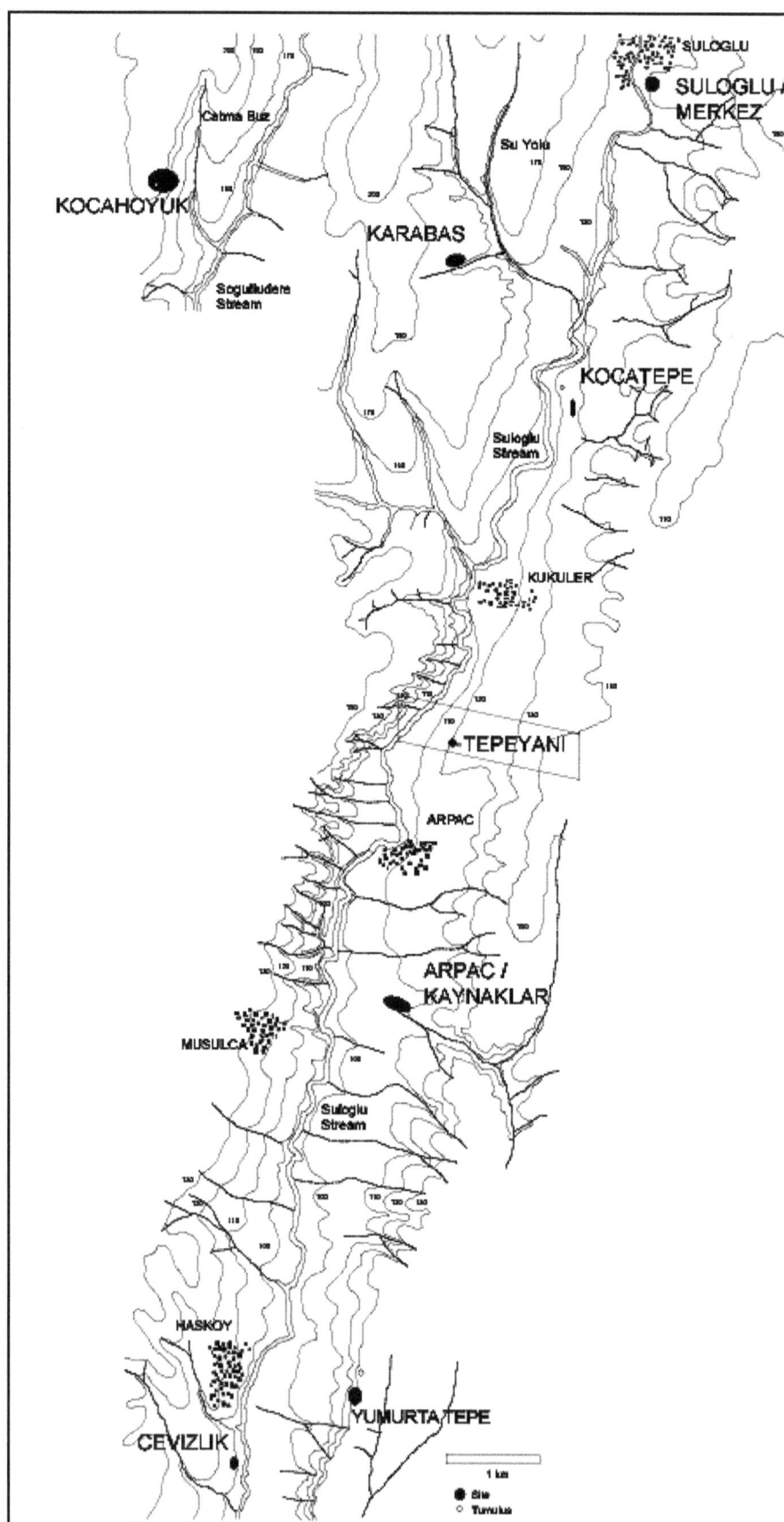

*Fig. I.4. Distribution of Prehistoric settlements in the Süloğlu Basin.
The box indicates area of intensive transect survey*

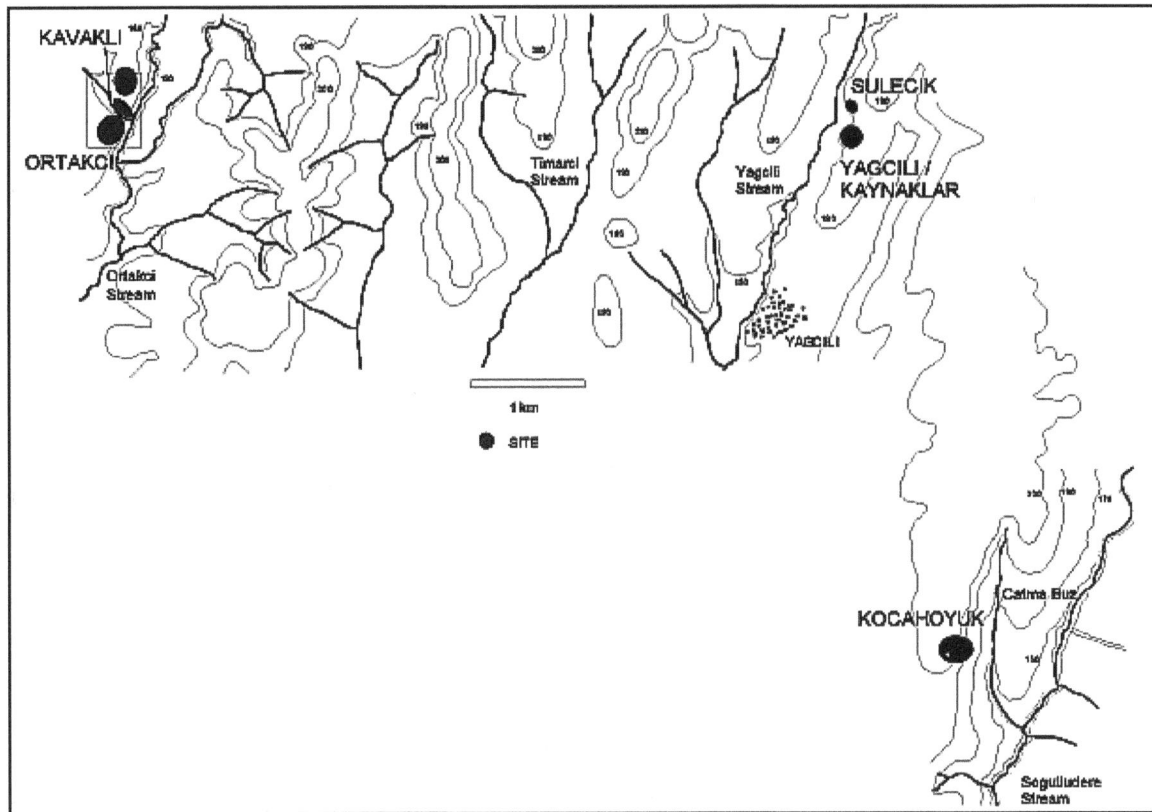

Fig. I.5. Distribution of Prehistoric settlements in the area along southern fringes of the Istranca Mountains. The box indicates area of intensive survey

Block and Transect Survey Results

KAVAKLI-ORTAKÇI AREA: The Kavaklı-Ortakçı area is situated south of the village of Kavaklı, on the west bank of the Çiftlik Stream, which is a tributary of the Iskenderköy. On the West bank of the stream, there is a small narrow gulch. An approximately 1x1 km square was investigated in the area. The main aim for the intensive survey in the Kavaklı-Ortakçı area was the very detailed mapping and recording of artefacts over the entirety of the survey area. The area consists of individual field-units. A total of 39 field-units of different shapes and dimensions were examined. Each walking line was divided into 10 m long individual mini-transects. The recorded artefacts density in each 10 m long field units gave us the limit of the site and the main concentrations of finds. During the extensive survey, our criterion for defining a site was a minimum of five artefacts per square meter. However, during the intensive survey, a different method was followed to define the approximate borders of a site, its main concentration and the off-site distribution. Now our criterion for defining a site border was a minimum of six artefacts in each "mini-transect". If there were more than ten artefacts, this would define the area as a site core. The core of each site was directly linked to topography. We observed finds concentrations on slight rises. Each find outside of the site border was taken as evidence of off-site activity. Three features could be defined here; the core of the site, the site distribution and the off-site distribution (*Fig. I.2*). In the Kavaklı-Ortakçı area, four single-period sites were discovered in the 1 x 1 km area. A total of 556 off-site artefacts was collected - 23 chipped stone implements, 1 spindle whorl and 532 sherds.

The whole Kavaklı-Ortakçı area was under cultivation with sunflowers and wheat and some fields were ploughed. The first part of survey was carried out in early summer, when the weather was always hot and cloudless, with no rain at all. The second part was carried out in early spring, when the weather was warm with light rain. In early summer, the height of the

9

wheat made surface collection impossible. Since the length of sunflowers was lower, the visibility in sunflower fields was excellent. At the end of the summer, after the harvest time, wheat fields allowed surface collection but visibility was still not excellent. The length of sunflowers was, by then, making surface collection difficult. However, surface visibility was still excellent. At the beginning, plough soil visibility was very poor. Visibility was undoubly improved by cleansing rainfall on fields ploughed in early spring. The surface team was charged with recording for each field, an estimate of its ground visibility, expressed as a percentage of the surface devoid of vegetation. Four terms was used for defining surface visibility; "best", "better than average", "worse than average" and "worst" (*Fig. I.6*). "Best" visibility (100-80%) covers sunflowers and bare fields; "better than average" (70-50%) covers ploughed fields; "worse than average" (40-20%) covers harvested wheat fields, and "worst" visibility (10-0%) covers wheat and corn fields. The variable effects of surface vegetation were always countered through the use of a "visibility count" in every field unit. For example, if the visibility in a field unit is "worst" and the sherd counted was four, we added other four to produce an accurate sherd density. If the visibility in a field-unit is "worse than average" and the sherd count was four, we added an extra two sherds.

The results of intensive survey in the Kavaklı-Ortakçı area showed that prehistoric settlements were marked by a series of abandonments and re-occupations (*Fig. I.7*). The Late Neolithic Kalojanovec-type of pottery is the earliest find to the south of the gulch. Chalcolithic settlements were situated to the north of the stream and are marked by Pre-Cucuteni / Maritsa (= Kocatepe) and Karanovo VI assemblages (see *Box B*). A Pre-Cucuteni / Maritsa (= Kocatepe) settlement was found just south of the village, far from the stream and the gulch. It is ca. 300 x 250 m in size. Single finds of Pre-Cucuteni / Maritsa (= Kocatepe) spread nearly as far south as the gulch. A Karanovo VI settlement is located ca.100-150 m southwest of the Pre-Cucuteni / Maritsa (= Kocatepe) settlement, close to the gulch. It is ca. 300 x 150 m in size and less than 1 m in height.

On the east bank of the Çiftlik stream, we found a small concentration characterized by Early Bronze Age I pottery together with two Pre-Cucuteni / Maritsa (= Kocatepe) and one Karanovo VI sherds. However, the sherds are scrappy and heavily worn. Thus it is not clear whether EBA I material constitute actual occupation or off-site activity. The Early Bronze Age II settlement was found on the south side of the gulch. It is ca. 250 m in diameter and ca. 5-6 m in height. Single finds of EBA II were found on the southern part of the settlements and also on the north side of the gulch. There is a hiatus in settlement between the Early Bronze Age II and the Late Bronze Age period. A settlement of the Late Bronze Age-Early Iron Age was found at the confluence of the stream and gulch. Single finds of the Late Bronze Age-Early Iron Age occurred to the south of the gulch. The Chalcolithic (Pre-Cucuteni / Maritsa (= Kocatepe) and Karanovo VI) settlements in the area were also investigated using 10 x 10 m grids.

Most of the off-site artefacts were very small, scrappy, and worn. The Chalcolithic (Pre-Cucuteni / Maritsa (= Kocatepe) sherds were easiest to recognise. They were thick, greyish in colour and sometimes decorated. However, some wares of the Pre-Cucuteni / Maritsa (= Kocatepe) and Karanovo VI periods were similar. Karanovo VI sherds were the most difficult to recognize, because small Karanovo VI and EBA sherds look similar. However, most of the EBA off-site artefacts were concentrated in particular areas. Early Iron Age sherds were also differentiated from other finds; deep black, low-fired and sometimes decorated, they were easy to recognize on the surface. To sum up, we can say 70% of off-site artefacts were securely dated. The remaining 30% should be dated to either the Chalcolithic or the Early Bronze Age.

The Chalcolithic, (Pre-Cucuteni / Maritsa (= Kocatepe) and Karanovo VI) periods give an off-site density of 1-3 sherds per "mini-transect" and an overall mean of 0.4 - 0.5 per 100 square meters. It is not clear that the EBA I material on the east bank of the Çiftlik stream constitute actual occupation or off-site activity. The EBA I gives an off-site density of 1-5 sherds per "mini-transect" and an overall mean of 1.2 sherds per 100 square meters. EBA II gives an off-site density of 1-5 sherds per "mini-transect" and an overall mean of 0.6 - 1.0 sherds per 100 square meters. The Late Bronze / Early Iron Age gives a off-site density of 1-2 sherds per "mini-transect" and an overall mean of 0.2 sherds per 100 square meter.

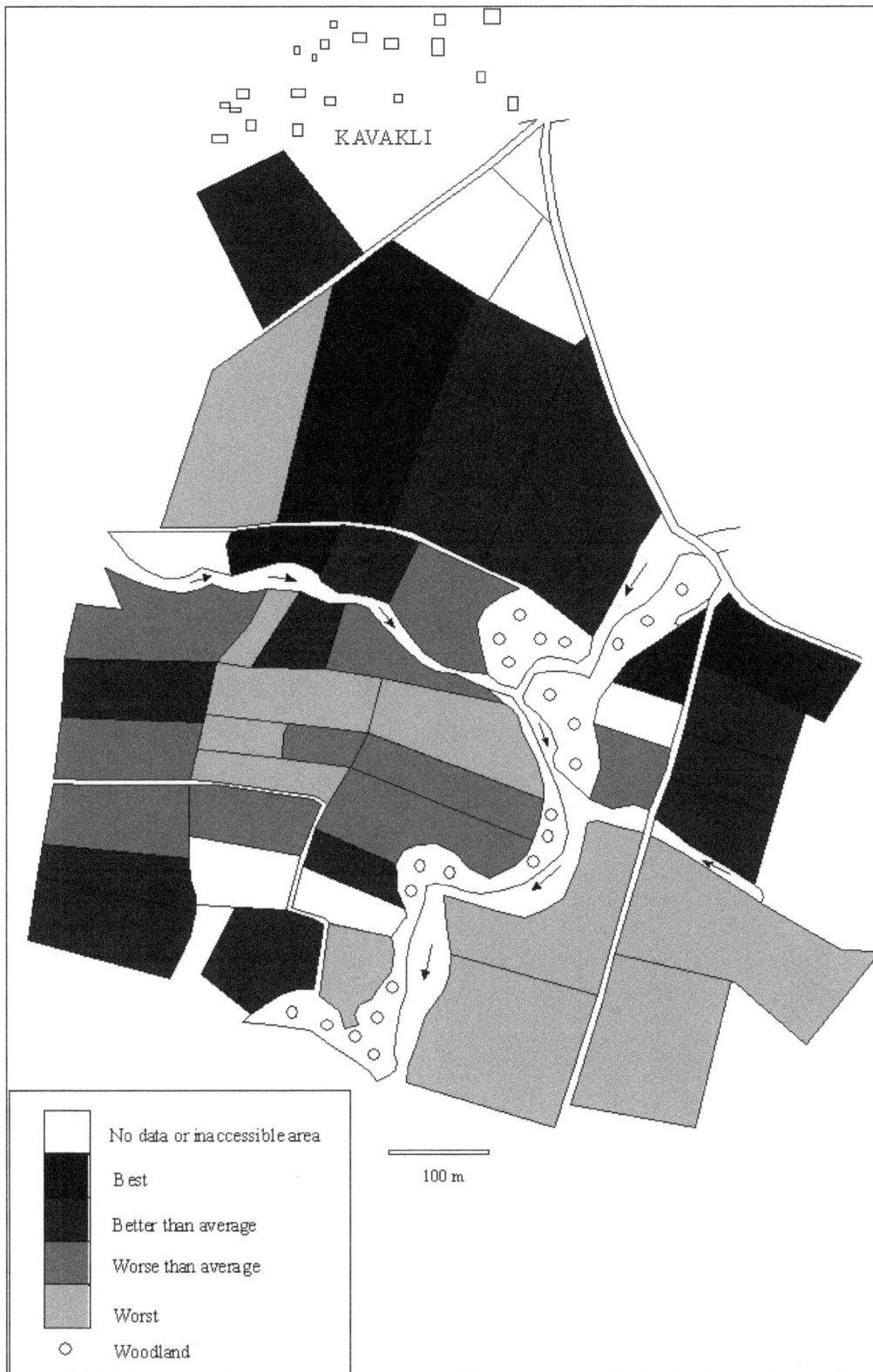

Fig. I.6. Relative ground visibility of fields in the Kavaklı-Ortakçı area

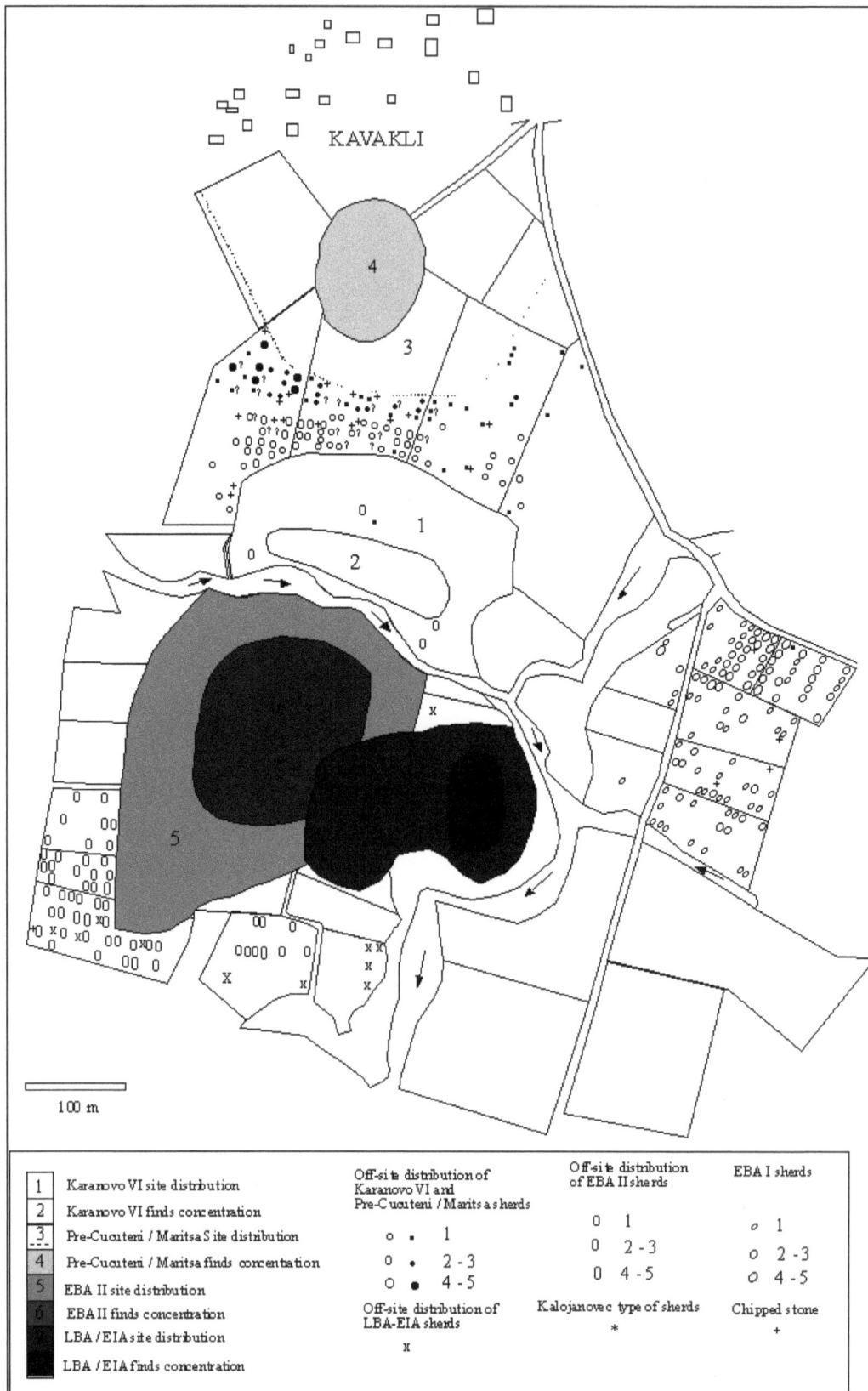

Fig. I.7. Distribution of sites and off-site finds in the Kavaklı-Ortakçı area

Single finds of Pre-Cucuteni / Maritsa (= Kocatepe) spread almost as far south as the gulch, extending to the east far another 100 m. Only two small sherds of Pre-Cucuteni / Maritsa (= Kocatepe) type were found on the East of the Çiftlik stream. The Karanovo VI single finds were found immediately around the settlement. Only one sherd was identified on the Eastern side of the Çiftlik stream. Because of poor visibility in the Eastern part of the Chalcolithic settlements, we have not recognized many off-site artefacts. The majority of EBA II single finds was found on the south-eastern side of the EBA II settlement. To the North of the gulch and the southern part of the EBA II settlement, there is an area with a far smaller number of finds. Although the visibility was "better than average" and "worse than average", we did not find a single sherd on the eastern part of the EBA II settlement.

Intra-site gridded survey: Kavaklı 1 and Kavaklı 2 were examined intensively, using both block and alternately-spaced 10 x 10 m quadrats. The results of the 10 x 10 m gridded survey enable the identification of the principal internal foci and boundaries of a site and give us a better understanding of its shape and extent. Artefacts collected from each grid were recorded on forms under the headings of pottery, chipped stone, stone axe, figurine etc. The intra-site gridded survey involved three distinct procedures. The first stage was to record the total number of sherds for each period, as well as the chipped stone for the whole site. This gave a good first impression as to the amount of dated material collected from the site and the number of chronological periods contained within it. The second stage was to put the number of artefacts of each period within each grid, and creating a grid-plan using computer programs. The third stage was to create a contour plan, using computer programs. That enabled a visual appreciation of the artefacts and a complex picture of the site.

Kavaklı 1 covers an area of ca. 300 x 150 m and finds are concentrated in an area some 200 x 80 m, spread over six different field units. Fields were cultivated by sunflowers and wheat and some fields were ploughed. With the exception of one field in the core, the visibility was "best" or "better than average" in all field units. The core of the settlement was investigated over an area of 100 x 50 m by a set of 24 10 x 10 m quadrats. During systematic field walking, it became clear that large quantities of archaeological material were concentrated in the western part of the site. This information led us to the choice of a survey grid of 5 x 5 m, covering almost the whole western field unit. Other field units in the core were sampled by alternate 10 x 10 m quadrats (*Fig. I.8*). The third field in the core was not investigated because of poor visibility. In Kavaklı 1, both prehistoric materials and Roman sherds were collected. All of the prehistoric material was dated to the Chalcolithic (Karanovo VI), period of the Balkans, comprising a total of 761 sherds and 51 chipped stone implements.

As a result of the 10 x 10 m grid survey, three distinct concentrations of material were observed - two in the northern part and one located in the eastern corner (*Fig. I.9*). Concentration 1 in the north gave a density of 70 sherds per 100 square meters falling to 40 sherds. Concentration 2 in the north gave density of 60 sherds per 100 square meters falling to 40 sherds. Very small fragments of daub were also noted in concentration areas as, well as a grinding stone and animal bones. Concentration 3 was located in the south-eastern corner, with a density of 50 sherds per 100 square meters, falling to 40 sherds. Most of the sampled area had an average of 30 sherds per 100 square meters. Sherd density gradually declined until 10 sherds per 100 square meters in the north-eastern corner. Most of the flint implements were found in the western part.

In Kavaklı 1, there is a strong contrast between sherd distribution and sherd weight. The main sherd weight is concentrated in the middle part of the sampled area, close with a density of 1.4 kg per 100 square meters, falling to 0.6 kg. Another concentration occurs in the north, with a density of 1 kg per 100 square meters (*Fig. I.10*). The differentiation between sherd distribution and sherd weight can be explained by a small number of very large sherds. The weight ratio in the concentration is 59.6 per 100 square meters, compared to an average ratio of 16 per 100 square meters in the sampled area.

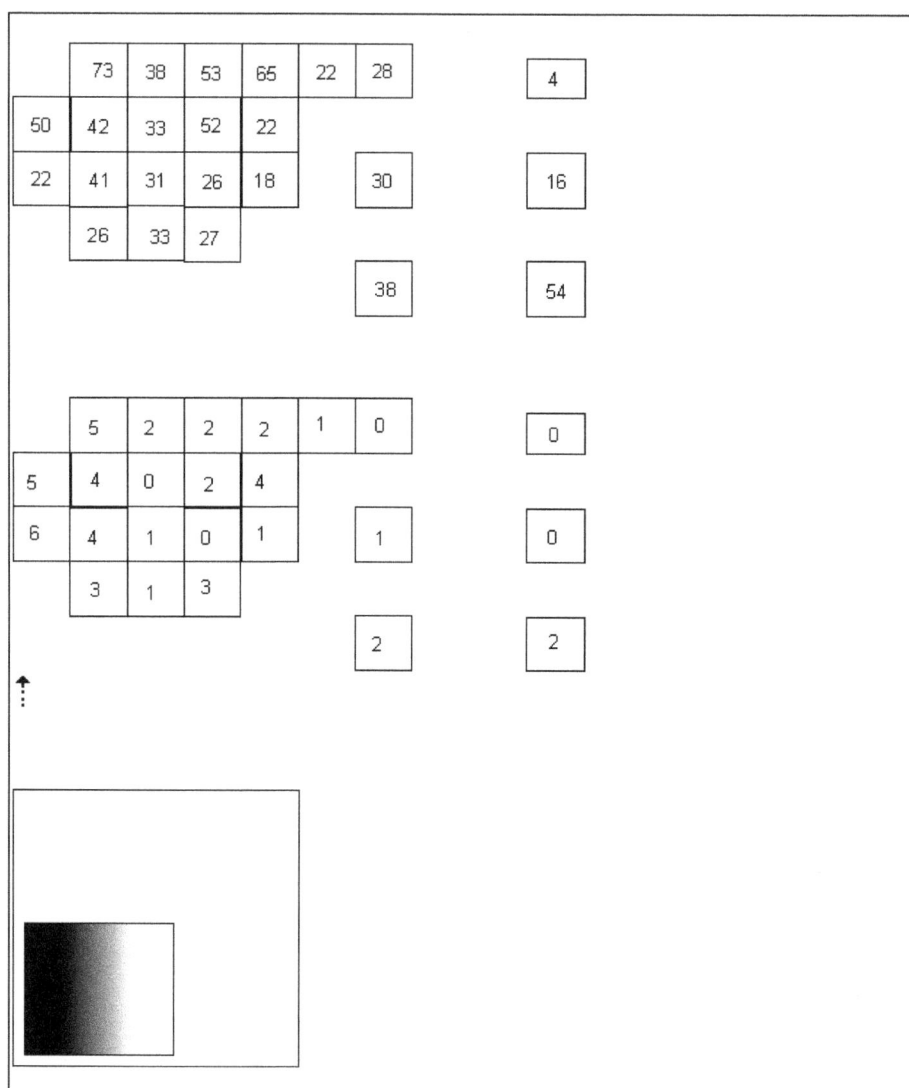

Fig. I.8. Kavaklı 1; (a) absolute sherd counts (b) chipped stone counts
(c) schematic model of sampling area

The prehistoric finds from Kavaklı 1 are homogeneous, suggesting a single phase of habitation. The concentration artefacts in Kavaklı 1 may be explained by a "site concentration" principle. The recorded artefact distribution indicates a multiple-focus concentration pattern. The residents who lived in a Balkan village kept their discarded objects in outside areas between and beyond their houses (Chapman 2000b). The discarded objects were ever-present, at least until they were trodden down into the ground surface. For a long period of time, residents were living in the discard surrounding their living area. The ethnographic data for discard concentration were also presented by Murray (1980). The house-unit with its discard creates very high finds concentrations. In Kavaklı, different foci of concentration may indicate the house-units.

Kavaklı 2 is approximately 250 x 250 m in size with a core of about 150 x 100 m. The Northern perimeter of settlement was probably destroyed by the modern village. Artefacts were observed right up to the edge of the village. The core of the site is divided into three field units. Fields were cultivated by sunflowers and wheat and some fields were ploughed. The visibility was "best" in only one field unit in the core and it was sampled with alternately spaced 14 10 x 10 m quadrats (*Fig. I.11*). All prehistoric material was dated to the Chalcolithic, Pre-Cucuteni / Maritsa (= Kocatepe), period of the Balkans. There were also a small number of Roman sherds. A total of 1443 sherds and 90 chipped stone implements was collected.

Kavakli 1

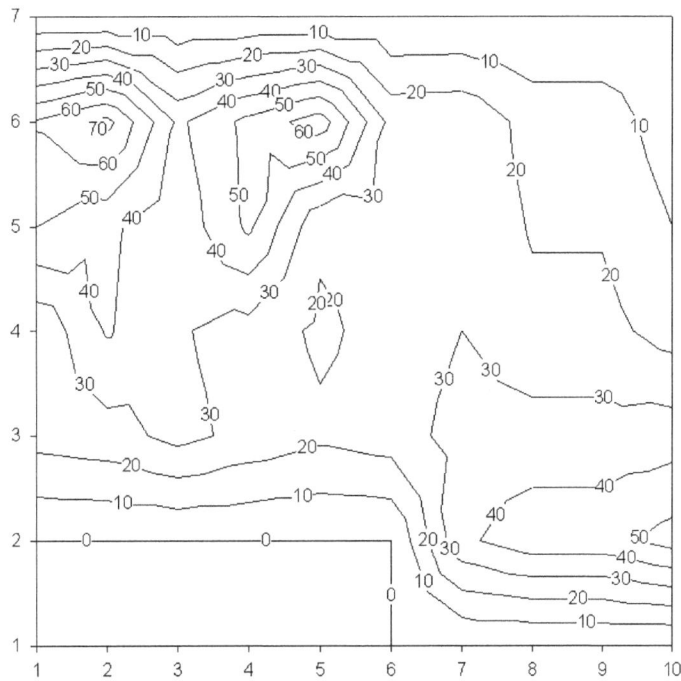

Fig. I.9. Interpolated contour plan of Kavaklı 1: Chalcolithic (Karanovo VI)
sherd distribution (density of sherds per 100 m²)

Kavakli 1

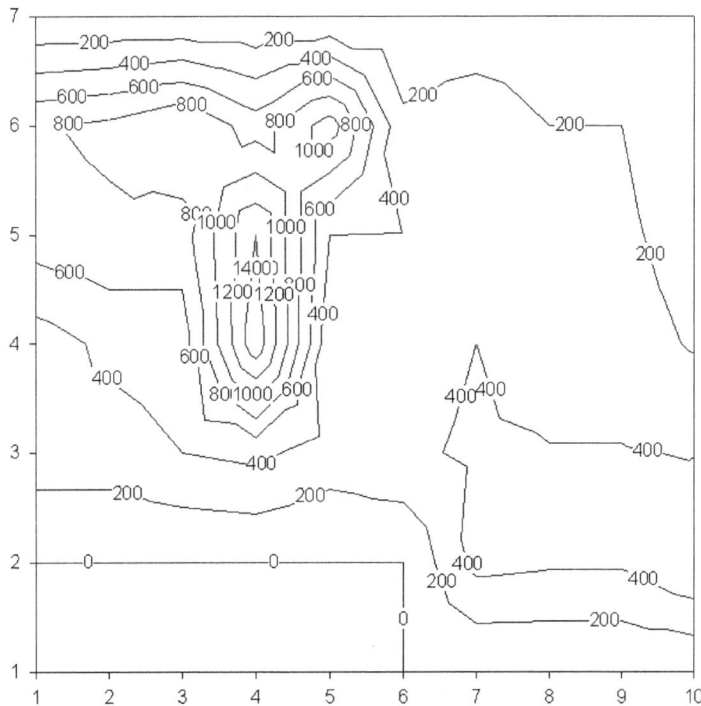

Fig. I.10. Interpolated contour plan of Kavaklı 1: Pottery weight

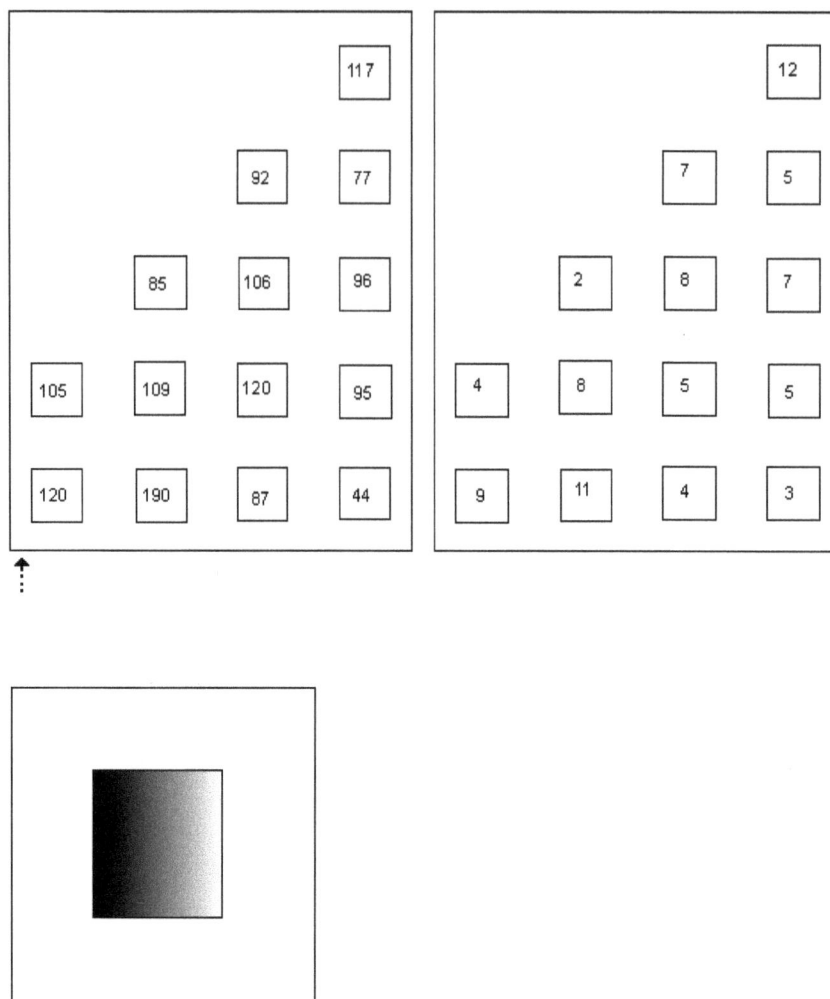

Fig. I.11. Kavaklı 2; (a) absolute sherd counts (b) chipped stone counts (c) schematic model of sampling area

In Kavaklı 2, there is one small concentration in the South-western part of the sampled area (*Fig. I.12*). It gives a density of 180 sherds per 100 square meters, falling to 120 sherds. Fragments of daub, a grinding stone, a stone axe and animal bones were also found in this concentration. On the other hand, most of the sampled area has a density of 100 sherds per 100 square meters. In Kavaklı 2, the Northern part of the core was not sampled; it is possible that more small concentrations exist.

The distribution pattern of Kavaklı 2 sherd weights matches the pattern of sherd density. The South-western concentration gives a density of 3 kg per 100 square meters, falling to 1.5 kg. Most of the sampled area gives a density average of 1.5 kg per 100 square meters, falling to 1 kg to the East (*Fig. I.13*).

The prehistoric finds from Kavaklı 2 are homogeneous, suggesting a single phase of habitation. There was only one small concentration recorded in Kavaklı 2. However, I assume that some small concentrations exist in the North. Southern concentration artefacts in Kavaklı 2 may be explained by the "site concentration" principle, as mentioned above. Artefact concentrations (sherds, bones, flints, an axe, a grinding stone and daub) in the South indicate the likelihood of a house-unit.

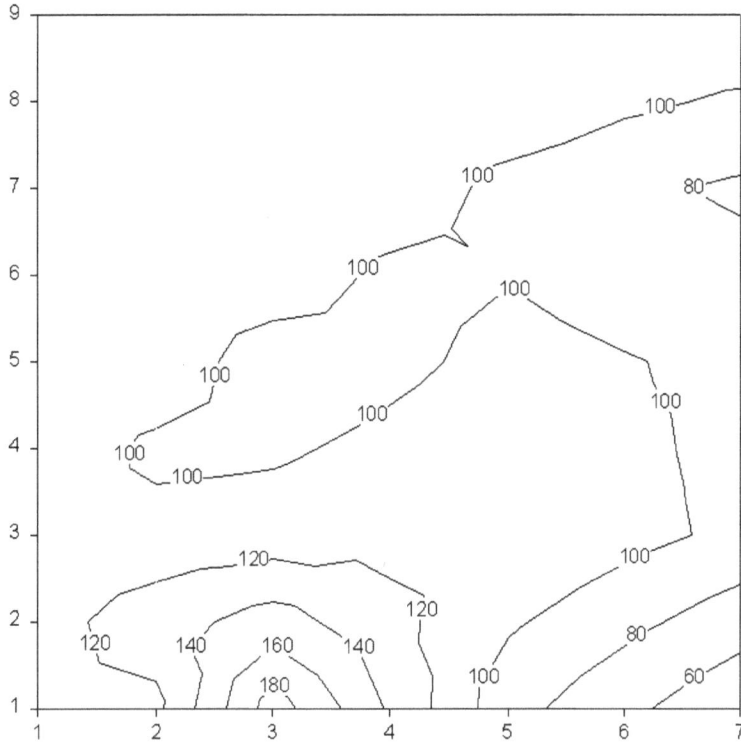

Fig. I.12. Interpolated contour plan of Kavaklı 2: Chalcolithic (Kocatepe)
sherd distribution (density of sherds per 100 m²)

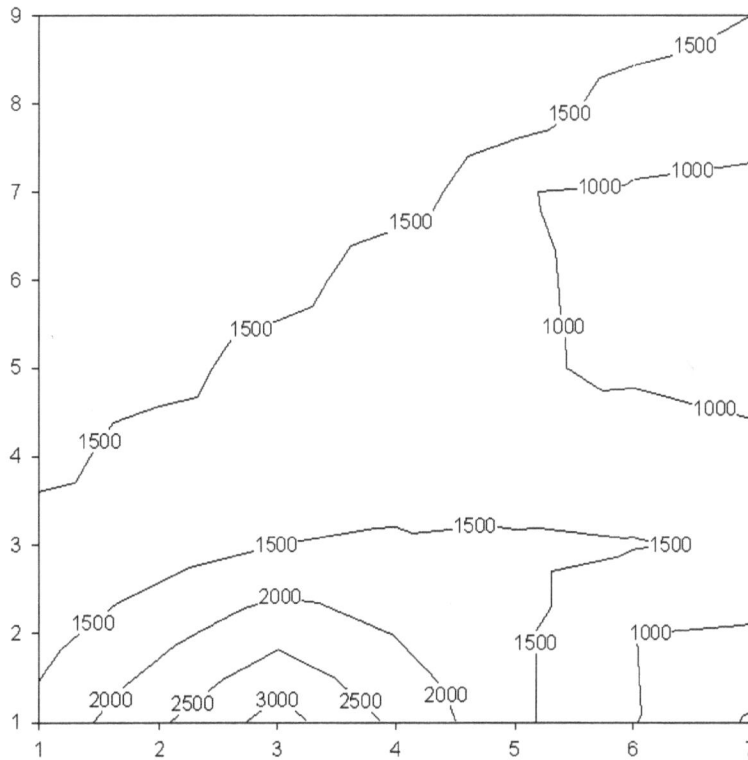

Fig. I.13. Interpolated contour plan of Kavaklı 2: Pottery weight

TEPEYANI-BAĞLARIÇI: The Tepeyanı-Bağlariçi area is located ca 1.5 km north of the village of Arpaç, on the eastern side of the Süloğlu Stream. Both sides of the Süloğlu valley are flanked by high and low terraces that are suitable for settlement and agriculture. The survey selected a transect, ca. 500 m wide and 1.4 km long, covering the high and low terraces and the floodplain.

There were four aims of the transect survey in the Tepeyanı-Bağlariçi area: 1. the examination of an area field by field; 2. the recording of artefacts over the entirety of the survey area; 3. the definition of site and off-site zones and the comparison of their finds and; 4. the definition of the chronological range of artefacts. In this area, a transect ca. 500 m wide and 1.4 km long was designed to cover different landscape units; the flood plain, low and high terraces and the upland. The flood-plain is 450 m wide while the lower and upper terraces are ca. 500 m wide. The upland is 200 m wide in this area. The surveyed area consists of 79 individual field-units of different shapes and dimensions. We used the same criteria for defining the site border, site concentration and off-site distribution as for the Kavaklı-Ortakçı area. In the Tepeyanı-Bağlariçi area, Chalcolithic and Late Bronze / Early Iron Age settlements were found only on the first terrace of the Süloglu Stream. A total of 36 off-site artefacts was collected - 10 chipped stone implements, 1 stone axe and 25 sherds.

The whole Tepeyanı- Bağlariçi area was under cultivation. As in the Kavaklı-Ortakçı area, fields were cultivated by sunflowers, wheat and corn and some fields were ploughed. Survey and weather conditions were similar to those of the Kavaklı-Ortakçı area. The surface visibility is shown in *Fig. I.14.*

The Chalcolithic settlement is marked by Pre-Cucuteni / Maritsa (= Kocatepe) and Karanovo VI assemblages. It is a small site ca. 80 x 60 m in size. The perimeter of the settlement has been damaged by the main Süloğlu-Havsa road. The Late Bronze / Early Iron Age settlement is more than 500 m long. Finds are concentrated in an area ca. 90 x 90 m in the north. In three different parts of the survey area, we found small concentrations of Hellenistic-Roman pottery. Four tumuli were recorded in the transect; three on the upland and one located on the first terrace, on the eastern side of the main road. Single finds, including Pre-Cucuteni / Maritsa (= Kocatepe), Iron Age pottery and chipped stone, were recorded in the transect (*Fig. I.15*). The Chalcolithic settlement was also investigated using 10 x 10 m grids.

The off-site artefacts were medium in size and only some of them were worn. Both the Chalcolithic (Pre-Cucuteni / Maritsa (= Kocatepe) and Late Bronze / Early Iron Age sherds were easily recognised. Pre-Cucuteni / Maritsa (= Kocatepe) sherds were thick, greyish coloured and sometimes decorated. Late Bronze / Early Iron Age sherds were black, low fired and sometimes decorated. In the Tepeyanı-Bağlariçi area, 100% of off-site artefacts were securely dated. Surprisingly, no Karanovo VI off-site artefacts were found. Karanovo VI finds on site are also low in density, ranging between 10 to 40 sherds per 100 square meters.

The Chalcolithic (Pre-Cucuteni / Maritsa (= Kocatepe) gives an off-site density of 0.06 - 0.14 sherds per 100 square meter. The Late Bronze / Early Iron Age gives an off-site density mostly of 0.06 sherds per 100 square meter. Most of the single finds were found on the low terrace. Only two pieces of Pre-Cucuteni / Maritsa (= Kocatepe) sherds and three flint implements were recorded on the high terrace, and only two pieces of Late Bronze / Early Iron Age sherds and one flint implement were found on the flood-plain.

Only six sherds of Late Bronze / Early Iron Age off-site pottery were found, immediately outside the settlement. On the other hand, with the exception of the settlement core, artefact density in this period is very low. The site distribution area of the settlement gives a mean density of 10-15 sherds per 100 square meters.

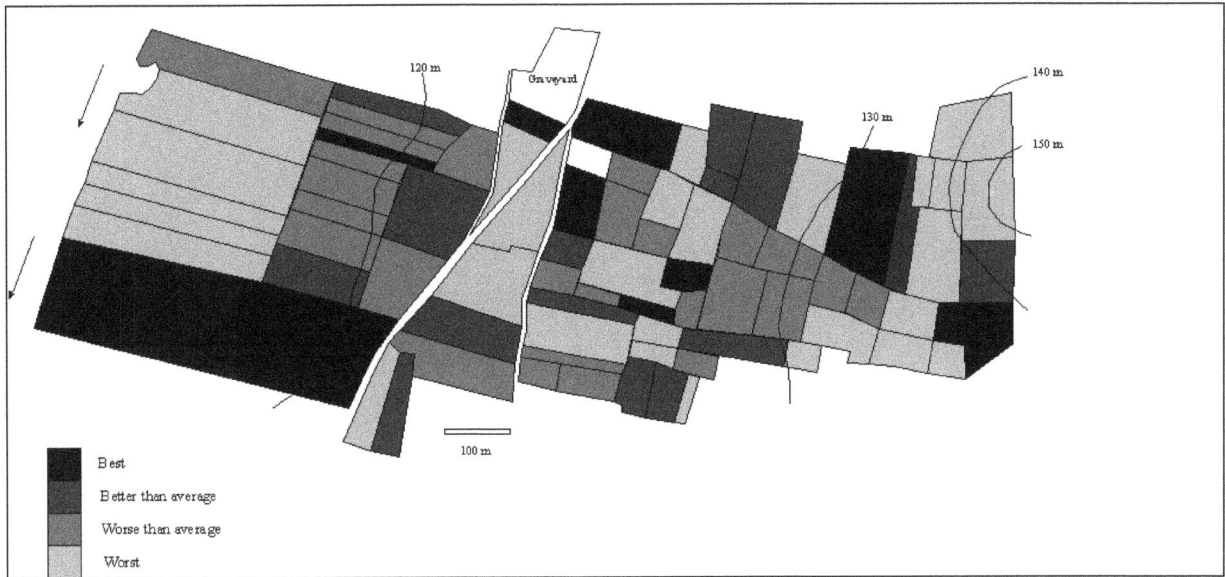

Fig. I.14. Relative ground visibility of fields in the Tepeyanı-Bağlariçi area

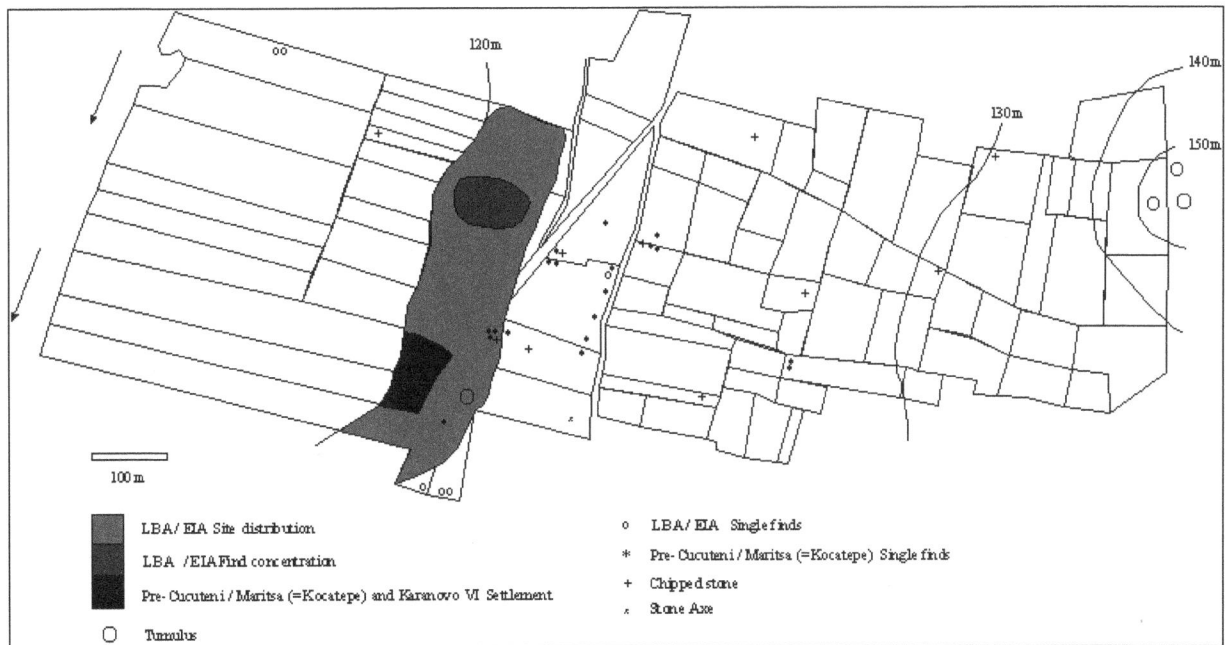

Fig. I.15. Distribution of sites and off-site finds in the Tepeyanı-Bağlariçi area

Intra-site gridded survey: Tepeyanı was examined intensively, using both block and alternately-spaced 10 x 10 m quadrates. An area of 70 x 40 m was examined intensively, using mainly a block of thirteen 10 x 10 m quadrats (*Fig. I.16*). This procedure gave us a better understanding of its shape and extent. The site covered two different field-units; both were ploughed and with "best" visibility. In Tepeyanı, Chalcolithic, Pre-Cucuteni / Maritsa (= Kocatepe) and Karanovo VI finds were recovered. Although a handful of Karanovo III pottery was present in early surveys, it was absent in intra-site gridded survey. The majority of finds was pottery; in addition, flint implements, two figurines, three stone axes and small fragments of daub were discovered. Most of the flint implements were found in the eastern side of the sampled area, in a similar concentration to that of the pottery. Although Tepeyanı is a small site, artefact density is very high. A total of 1010 sherds and 56 chipped stone implements was collected.

The survey results show us a single concentration pattern of artefacts. A high density of artefacts was found near the main road, with fall-off at regular intervals (*Fig. I.17*). The concentration of Pre-Cucuteni / Maritsa (= Kocatepe) settlement gives a density of 80 sherds per 100 square meter falling off at regular intervals to 20 sherds. The main concentration of Karanovo VI settlement gives a density of 40 sherds per 100 square meters, falling off at almost regular intervals to 10 sherds (*Fig. I.18*).

The pattern of sherd weights matches the pattern of sherd density. The main concentration of sherd weight gives a density of 2 kg per 100 square meters falling off at regular intervals to 0.5 kg (*Fig. I.19*).

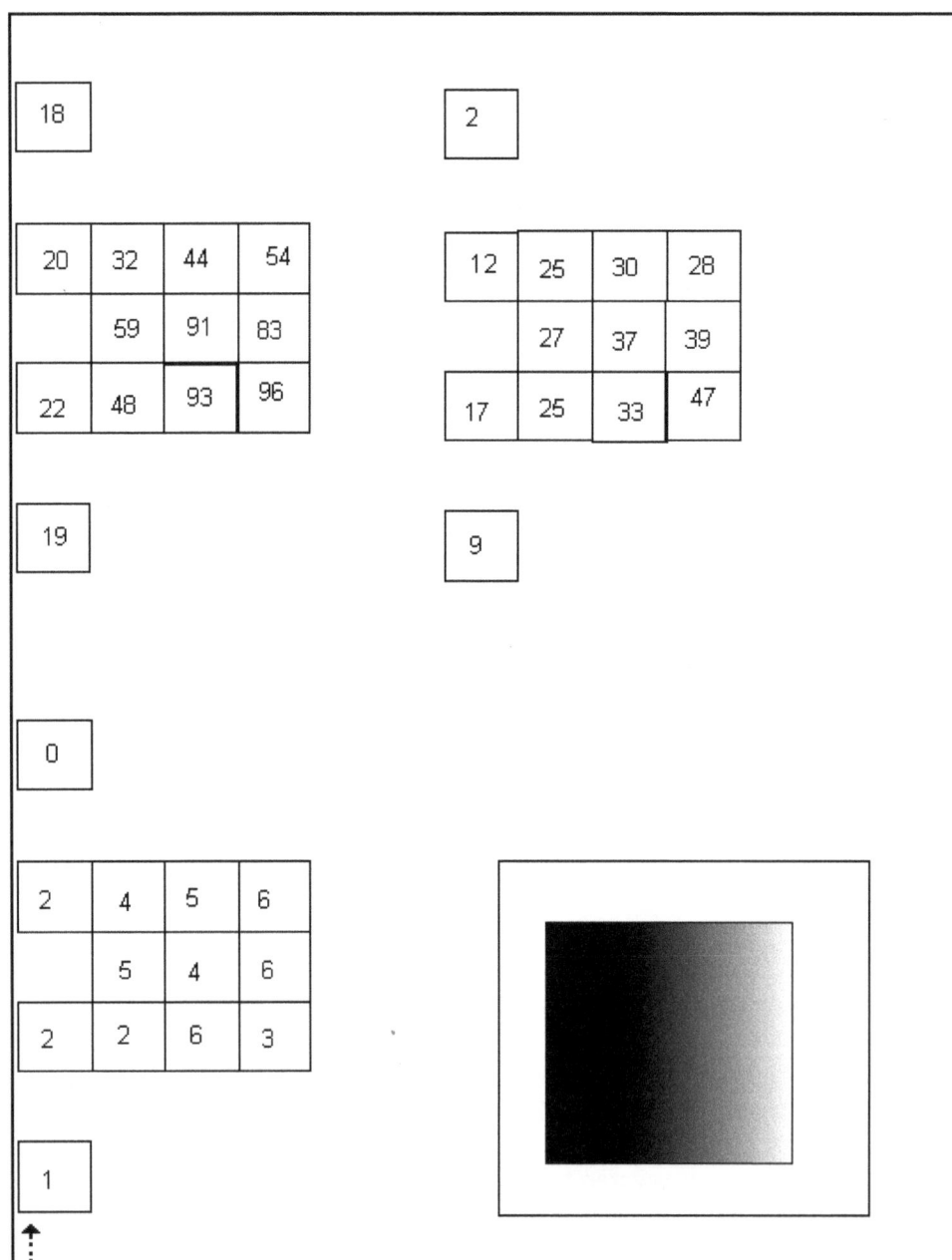

Fig. I.16. Tepeyanı; (a-b) absolute sherd counts (c) chipped stone counts
(d) schematic model of sampling

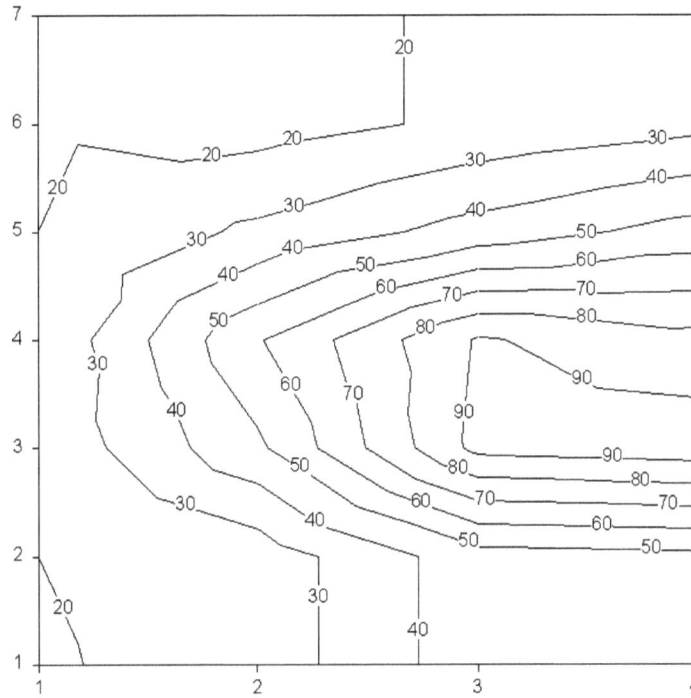

Fig. I.17. Interpolated contour plan of Tepeyanı:
Chalcolithic (Kocatepe) sherd distribution (density of sherds per 100 m²)

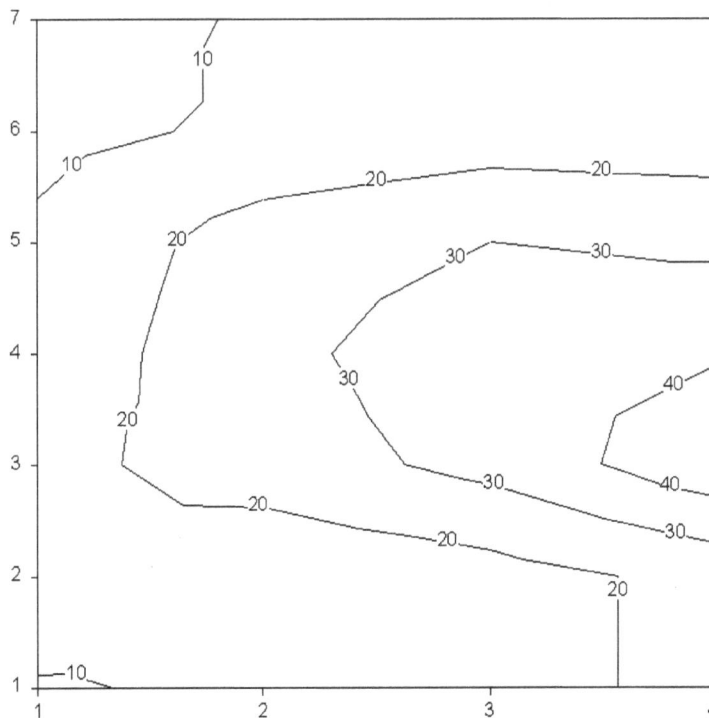

Fig. I.18. Interpolated contour plan of Tepeyanı: Chalcolithic (Karanovo VI)
sherd distribution (density of sherds per 100 m²)

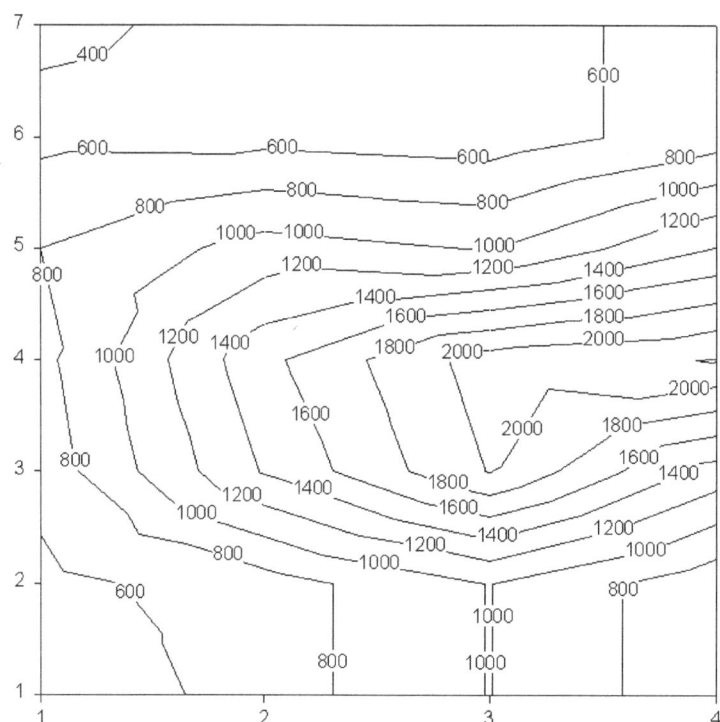

Fig. I.19. Interpolated contour plan of Tepeyanı: Pottery weight

Tepeyanı shows a single-focus concentration pattern. The explanation of such a central concentration at Tepeyanı can be explained in three different ways. First, Tepeyanı is located on a first terrace of the Süloğlu Stream, as mentioned above. The first terrace of stream has a gentle slope on which the site formed. In Tepeyanı, it seems that the artefacts are generally larger and heavier than the soil matrix. Sediments are being washed down slope by the rain and artefacts are left in position. This can result in a "concentration effect" on the surface density of material (Cherry *et. al* 1991:204).

Secondly, the perimeter of the settlement has been damaged by the main road. During road construction, it is probable that artefacts were cleared to the side of the road, resulting in a secondary concentration near the road.

Thirdly, as Chapman (2000b) argues, the residents who lived in a Balkan village put their discarded objects and food remains together with midden-like discard not always into "rubbish pits" but also outside areas between and beyond their houses. The discarded objects were ever-present, at least until they were trodden down into the ground surface. For a long period of time, residents were living in this discard surrounding their living area (cf. Murrey 1980; Hayden and Cannon 1983). According to Chapman, this principle reaches its apogee on settlements, where the basic principle is one of living where the ancestors had lived (Chapman 2000b). House units producing a high density of discard objects may result in a "concentration effect" on the surface density. On open sites, the land between houses was divided up between households, often as gardens. The house order and discard quantity on the settlement may be reflected on the surface as a large single concentration with fall-off regular intervals. When house units are set close to each other, producing a high density of discard, this may be reflected on the surface as a large single concentration. Without excavation, it is difficult to decide which is the best explanation of the single concentration pattern at Tepeyanı.

BOX B - Culture and Time

The concept of the "archaeological cultures" has been discussed by different archaeologist over a long period of time (e.g. Childe 1957; Binford and Binford 1968; Clark 1968; Klejn 1982; Daniel and Renfrew 1988; Hodder 1982b; 1982c). The Childean concept of cultures concerns regularly associated artefact assemblages found within a limited geographical area (Childe 1929). According to Childe, the people producing a culture were only definable by the material culture itself (Childe 1957). The culture was a purely archaeological entity. D. Clarke echoes this definition and, like Childe, he saw material culture as representing coded survival information passed from generation to generation. According to Clarke, an archaeological culture is a polythetic set of specific and comprehensive artefact types which consistently recur together in assemblages within a limited geographic area (Clarke 1968). L. Binford (1968) claimed that there was a direct linkage between cultural systems and material culture, because of the interaction between normative ideas, behaviour and material remains. For Binford, culture was the extra-somatic means of adaptation for the human organism - a non-genetic response to local environmental change (Binford 1972). C. Renfrew took up this theme in his characterisation of culture as an essentially homeostatic device to ensure both minimum changes in the system and adaptations to fluctuations in the external environment (Renfrew 1972). A post-processual view was given by Hodder, according to which, each culture is a particular historical product, to be understood as a meaningful framework for cultural action rather than as an adaptation to the physical and social environment (Hodder 1982c). Material culture comprises 'a structured set of differences, the product of human categorisation processes in dialectical relationship to human action' (Hodder 1982c). Since artefacts are immediately cultural and not social, they can inform on society only through an adequate understanding of the cultural context (Hodder 1982c).

The term "culture", which I am going to use in this book is similar to Clarke and Hodder, which is a collection of archaeologically observable data; it is defined as the regularly occurring assemblage of associated artefacts, which used in an active manner to display in symbolic form, feeling of allegiance and defence etc, and regarded in this sense as indicative of the cultural identity of a particular social group.

There are certain differences in terminology between the Balkans and Anatolia. In the Balkan terminology, the Early Neolithic period correlates to Late Neolithic / Early Chalcolithic period of Anatolia. The Middle Chalcolithic of Anatolia correlates to both Middle and Late Neolithic period of the Balkans, and the Late Chalcolithic of Anatolia correlates whole (Early, Middle and Late) Chalcolithic period of the Balkans. On the other hand, in Greek terminology, the Chalcolithic period generally is called the Final Neolithic. Geographically, Eastern Thrace is a part of the Balkans, and most of Eastern Thrace material is close to the Balkan material. So, in this study, Balkan terminology is preferred.

The Early Neolithic period in Eastern Thrace shows two different regional and cultural zones: 1. The Southern part of Eastern Thrace is characterized by the Western Anatolian early Neolithic tradition. The early Neolithic sites in this region, such as Hoca Çeşme, Hamaylıtarla and Kaynarca (*Fig. B.1*), indicate that the Western Anatolian red slipped and burnished ware tradition extended in this area (Erdoğu 2000; 2002). 2. The Eastern part, as well as the inner part of Eastern Thrace is characterized by the Fikirtepe Culture (Özdoğan 1997; 1999a). The Fikirtepe Culture is the earliest Neolithic culture in northeast Anatolia. It is proposed that the origins of the Fikirtepe Culture are located in Central Anatolia (Özdoğan 1989:203; 1997:22; 1999b:215-216; Thissen 1999:37). Fikirtepe sherds were found at Bulgar Kaynağı and Aşağı Pınar in the upper Ergene basin (Özdoğan 1999b: 214). Yarımburgaz Cave layers 5 and 4 were also dated to the Fikirtepe Culture (Özdoğan 1997). According to C14 dates, early layers of Hoca Çeşme can be dated ca. 6500-6000 cal BC (Thissen 2002; Erdoğu *et al.* 2003), while the

Fikirtepe Culture can be dated ca. 6460-5500 cal. BC (Thissen 2002; Erdoğu *et al.* 2003). An Early Neolithic settlement with Hoca Çeşme material was also found on the island of Gokceada (Harmankaya and Erdoğu 2003). Bulgarian prehistory is dominated by tell Karanovo, one of the largest tells in the Nova Zagora plain. Karanovo I and II layers are dated to the Early Neolithic period ca. 6000/5900 - 5500/5450 cal. BC (Boyadziev 1995: Table.4). Karanovo I and II layers were also found in Aşağı Pınar (Özdoğan 1999b:220). Typical Karanovo I pottery as well as lithic technology was also found at Hoca Çeşme layer 2 (Özdoğan 1997; 1998b).

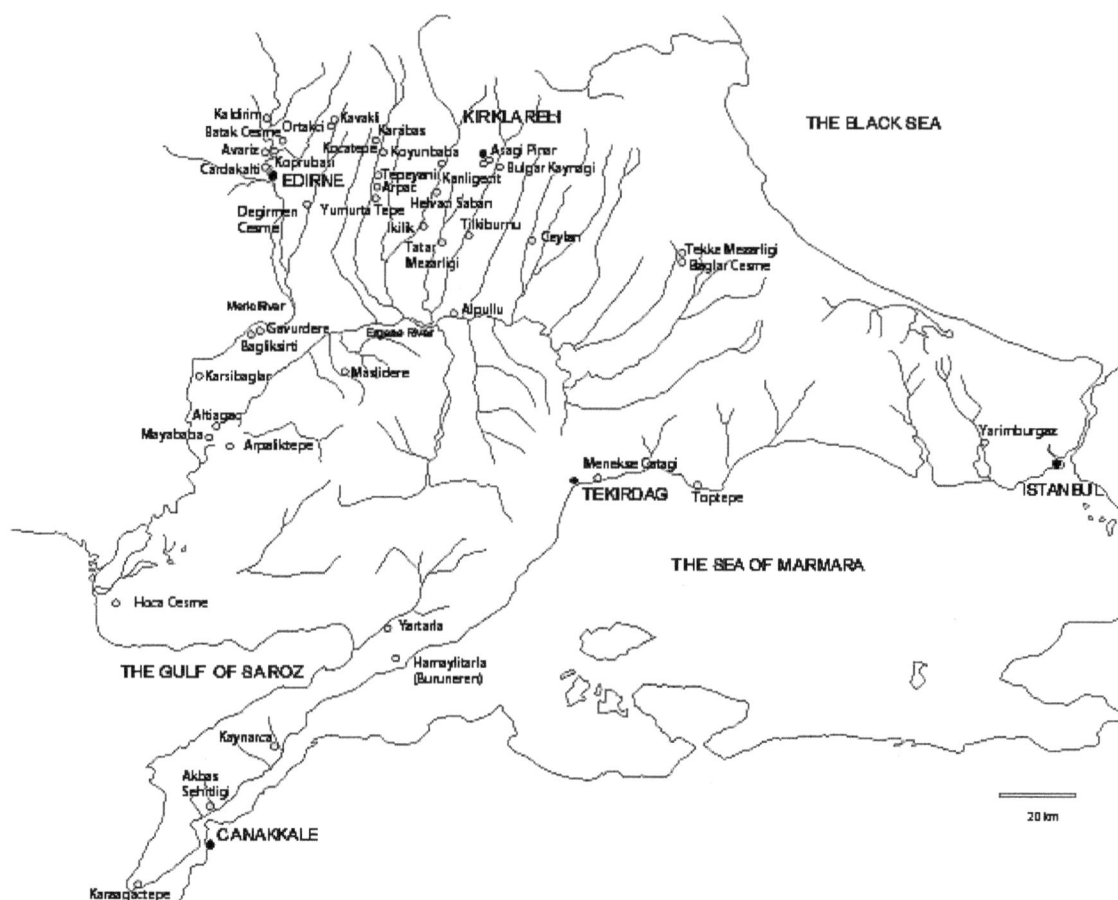

Fig. B.1. Neolithic and Chalcolithic sites of Eastern Thrace

The Middle Neolithic period of Eastern Thrace is represented by the Karanovo III-Vesselinovo culture of the Balkans. Karanovo III-Vesselinovo settlements were found in the Meriç and Ergene basins of Eastern Thrace. The existence of Karanovo III material in Greek Thrace and Macedonia indicates that this culture extends over a large geographical area. Among the Karanovo III-Vesselinovo settlements, Aşağı Pınar, Altıağaç, Köprübaşı and Gavurdere are noteworthy (*Fig. B.1*). There is no evidence of Karanovo III-Vesselinovo settlements in the Northern shore of the Sea of Marmara, except at Yarımburgaz cave. A few Karanovo III sherds were found in unstratified deposits at Yarımburgaz (Özdoğan *et al.* 1991:74). Boyadziev give dates of 5500/5450 - 5200/5100 cal. BC for Karanovo III (Boyadziev 1995: Table.4).

The Late Neolithic period of Eastern Thrace is marked by different cultural complexes. The Southern part is represented by the Toptepe culture. The site of Toptepe is located on the Northern shore of the Sea of Marmara (*Fig. B.1*). The Toptepe pottery is characterized by two distinct ware types - micaceous and coarse (Özdoğan *et al.* 1991). The micaceous ware is white mica-tempered with dull burnish. Surface colours are in tones of dark grey and black. The most common form is a tall-necked carinated jar, usually with a strap handle and with shallow incised decoration (Özdoğan *et al.* 1991: Fig.22; 9). The coarse ware has roughened exterior surfaces with nail, wedge or stroke impressions, applied-bands with finger impressions or applied lumps of clay. The interior surfaces, however, are smoothed or slightly burnished. The most common shape is a rounded bowl, sometimes with carination. The Toptepe coarse ware was found at Hoca Çeşme layer 1 (Özdoğan 1993: 183; Özdoğan 1998b), unstratified deposits of Yarımburgaz cave (Özdoğan et al. 1991: Fig.14;3-4), and Tekke Mezarlığı and Bağlar Çeşme in the Vize plain (Özdoğan 1995a: 531). The Toptepe micaceous ware was found at Alpullu, on the Northern side of the Ergene River (Mansel 1938:22-23), and at Arpaç / Kaynaklar in the Tunca basin (Erdoğu 2002). The Toptepe pottery was also found at Aşağı Pınar 3, together with Karanovo III-IV pottery (Özdoğan 1998a:75). On the other hand, the coarse ware of Toptepe seems to occur at the Karanovo III-IV settlements in Southeast Bulgaria (e.g. Drama: Lichardus et al. 2000: Taf.26;8,13). On the basis of C14 dates the Toptepe culture can be dated to ca. 5300-4900 cal. BC.

Karanovo III-IV (Early IV) pottery has been found in the Edirne and Kırklareli regions. The Karanovo III-IV culture contains Toptepe elements in Eastern Thrace. Our knowledge is essentially based on the excavation results from Aşağı Pınar. In Aşağı Pınar, layer 3 can be dated Karanovo III-*IV* period, and immediately follows layer 4 (Özdoğan 1998a: 74-75). According to uncalibrated C14 dates, layer 3 was dated ca. 6300-6200 BP (Özdoğan 1998a: 75), ca. 5200 cal. BC. The western part of Eastern Thrace is represented by the Maslıdere culture. Surface finds indicates that Maslıdere pottery is close to Toptepe (Erdoğu 1999a; 2002). Although the fabric and decorative techniques of Maslıdere pottery seem similar to Toptepe, the motifs are different. Also missing in the sites of Maslıdere culture are the micaceous wares of Toptepe. There are, as yet, no excavations of Maslıdere settlements. So far, no Maslıdere pottery was found either in Bulgaria or Greece.

At the end of the Late Chalcolithic period, the Bulgarian Kalojanovec type of pottery was found together with Çardakaltı type of local pottery in a number of settlements in the Edirne region. Çardakalti pottery is characterised by two distinct wares- buff or reddish buff coloured ware and black burnished ware. The first is characterised by grooved wavy lines, combined with triangular dot impressions, and the second is characterised by white paint (Erdoğu 2002). No Çardakaltı pottery was found in the Balkans and Anatolia. During this period, the Beşiktepe-Kumtepe Ia culture of Western Anatolia extended to the Gelibolu peninsula, and probably to the whole Southern part of Eastern Thrace (e.g. Toptepe: Özdoğan et al. 1991 ; Akbaş Sehitliği: French 1964).

The early stage of the Chalcolithic period is represented by the Kocatepe culture. All Kocatepe settlements have been discovered in the Upper Ergene basin. The pottery evidence indicates that the Kocatepe culture is a local culture in Eastern Thrace which is closely related to the Maritsa, Sava and Pre-Cucuteni cultures in the Balkans (Erdoğu 2002). However, there is, as yet, no excavated Chalcolithic site in Eastern Thrace. This culture extended the Harmanlı area of Southeast Bulgaria (Leshtakov 1997) on its west side and the Vize-Saray plain on its East side. There were no Kocatepe settlements found in the lower Ergene basin. The Maritsa culture of the Balkans can be dated to ca. 4900/4850 - 4600/4550 cal. BC (Boyadziev 1995), while the Pre-Cucuteni culture can be dated to ca 5050-4600 cal. BC (Mantu 1998:183).

The Late Chalcolithic period of Eastern Thrace is marked by a decrease in the number of settlements. Only a few sites were discovered in the upper Ergene basin, and are relatively small. It seems likely that the pottery from Eastern Thrace was the product of local development with closely related to the Kodjadermen- Gumelniţa-Karanovo VI and the Krivodol-Salcuţa-Bubanj cultures (Erdoğu 1999b; 2002). The Kodjadermen-Gumelniţa-Karanovo VI culture as well as the Krivodol-Saltuca-Bubanj culture can be dated to ca. 4500/4400-4100/3800 cal. BC (Boyadziev 1995).

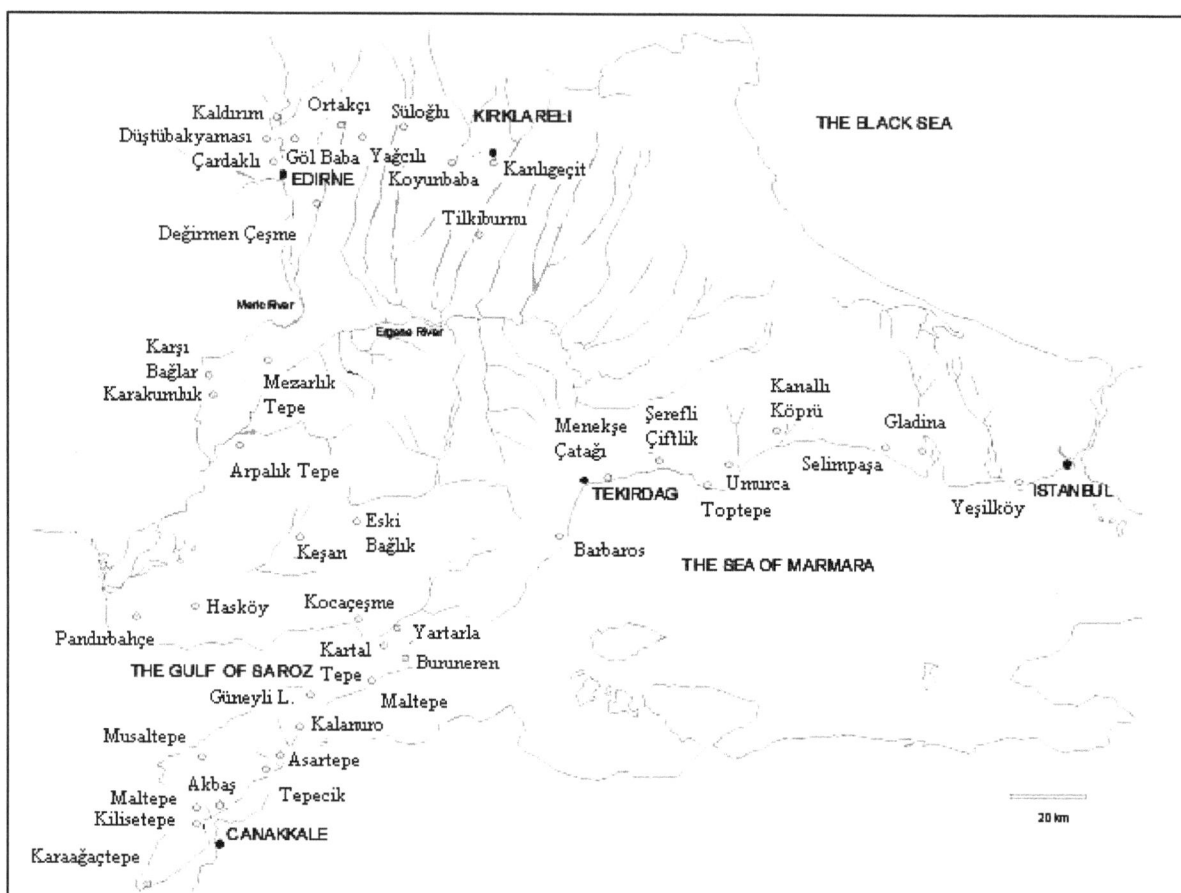

Fig. B.2. Early Bronze Age Sites of Eastern Thrace (Turkish Thrace)

The Early Bronze Age of Eastern Thrace is marked by an increase in the number of settlements (*Fig. B.2*). A total of 57 Early Bronze Age sites were noted in Eastern Thrace (Harmankaya and Erdoğu 2002). It is characterized by two different zones; the littoral (the Gelibolu Peninsula and the Northern shore of the Sea of Marmara) and the interior (the Ergene basin). The interior is marked by flat settlements rather than tells. The Early Bronze Age tells occur mostly in the littoral zone. There are also cultural differences between the interior and the littoral zones. The Early Bronze Age tells in the Gelibolu Peninsula are related to the Bronze Age sequences of Kumtepe Ib and Troy I in Western Anatolia (Kılıç 2000). The pottery from Tells in the Northern shore of the Sea of Marmara was the product of local development which is closely related to the Kumtepe/Troy sequences (Kılıç 2000). The pottery on interior settlements is the repertoire of Ezero-Yunatsite-Mihalich type. On the basis of Kanligeçit excavations, Özdoğan (1998a; 1999a) suggests that at the end of the Early Bronze Age, some Anatolian-sponsored colonies settle on Thracian territory. Kanligeçit consists of an acropolis and a lower town, date to the Early Bronze III. A series of megara with stone foundations inside a fortification wall was discovered (Özdoğan 1998a; 1999a). The construction technique, hitherto unattested in the region and the associated pottery points to connections with the Troas and west-central Anatolia. This megaron phase was found immediately on top of an Early Bronze level with Balkan sherds belonging to the Ezero period. There are, as yet, no known Middle Bronze Age settlements in Eastern Thrace. The Late Bronze Age and the Early Iron Age is marked by an increase in the number of settlements, especially in the Edirne-Kirklareli region. The Early Iron Age of Eastern Thrace is characterised by megalithic monuments. In Eastern Thrace, megalithic monuments such as dolmens and standing stone complexes are located on the Istranca Mountains. Only detailed excavation was conducted at the dolmen of Arpalık, Lalapaşa (Akman 1997). Sealed funerary deposit from within the middle chamber consists of human bones of four individuals. The Early Iron Age and Hellenistic potteries, spindle-whorls and a fibula were found inside the chambers.

Interpreting off-site artefacts

Single finds or minor concentration of finds in a landscape, around the settlements may be explained by several processes such as, manuring, seasonal use field huts or facilities, field cooking and eating, manufacturing, rubbish management, artefact preparation and ceremonial locales etc.

Wilkinson has argued that artefact discards around the Near Eastern settlements were associated with agricultural activities, mainly manuring (Wilkinson 1982: 324). According to Wilkinson, such enterprises incorporated a miscellany of artefacts into manure and all but the largest of these artefacts would eventually be spread on the fields as part of manure. This artefact discard is a continuous process through time. Gaffney and Tingle also agree that artefact discard in surrounding individual settlements should therefore, in some circumstances, define a minimum economic area associated with that site (Gaffney and Tingle 1989: 216). Hence, the presence of large amounts of pottery in the fields around a settlement is associated with manuring activities (Gaffney et. al. 1991; Gaffney and Tingle 1989: 224). The manure probably originated from the settlement, where it was contaminated or mixed with household refuse before being spread on the fields (Bintliff and Snodgrass 1988). On the other hand some archaeologists such as Neústupný claim that in prehistoric times, manuring would hardly bring any objects to the fields (1998: 56). But he does not explain why this should be. Prehistoric people, at least in some areas, improved the quality of their fields by transporting sods from their residential area. Such sods could contain sherds and other finds. Minor activity foci were less intensively used then the normal permanent occupation site and 'the mythical donkey off whose back pots are supposed to have fallen' (Bintliff and Snodgrass 1988). Bintliff also argues that the number and degree of material and character of the material can affect the interpretation of off-site artefacts (Bintliff 2000).

Archaeologists studying more complex societies have paid little attention to the idea of a minimum economic area associated with settlements. Flannery, who worked on semi-sedentary farming communities in the Tehuacan valley, Mexico, noted that there are temporary camps some distance from a permanent village (Flannery 1976). Minor concentration of finds around the settlements may be explained by short-lived farm sites or seasonal use temporary field huts.

Single finds or minor concentration of finds outside settlements may also be explained by rubbish management (Foard 1978: 363; Hayes 1991). The simplest mechanism for getting rid of refuse is throwing it away or burying it in the immediate vicinity of dwellings or a particular area (Needham and Spence 1997). If refuse is deposited outside settlements, they will create a more or less a horizontal layer. If this layer was destroyed by erosion and ploughing, finds would have been spread over a large area.

Cooking, eating, drinking, food-sharing and food-giving provide the basis for social relationships in societies. During harvest time, cooking and eating may have occurred in the field. Ceremonial activities may also have occurred in the field (cf. Zuni ceremonies: Persons 1919: 285). Thus some single finds may be explained by social or ceremonial activities.

A number of factors related to natural transport and post-depositional disturbance should also take into consideration for artefact distributions in the landscape. Individual artefacts are removed from their context by rain and wind process, erosion, burrowing animals, root action, and human activity - kicking, scuffing, trampling and especially ploughing. Thus this makes it difficult to interpret surface artefacts. Observation of surface artefacts on ploughing sites showed that sherds planted in the immediate subsoil undergo significant lateral displacement within several years (Roper 1976; Ammerman 1985). Roper's ploughsoil experiments show that, after two or three decades of ploughing, artefacts may be displaced by anything between 20 cm and 10 m (Roper 1976). A. Ammerman's experiments in southern Italy suggest that, by the end of six or more ploughing episodes, a tile moved vary between 1.18 m and 1.74 m. Many tiles moved no further than 2 m of their starting position (Ammerman 1985: 38).

A number of factors, such as the type of agriculture, the nature of the soil and the landscape topography can affect artefact movement (Bintliff and Snodgrass 1988; Clark and Schofield 1991). In an arid environment with light soils, artefact movement may be less than in a temperate climate, where heavier soils predominate (Clark and Schofield 1991: 94). Smaller material on sloping surfaces tended to move further than larger material on flat surfaces. The poor condition or low numbers of sherds may also make difficult to make a chronologically or spatial separation between artefacts. Erosion is not only one of the most important factor of artefact exposure, but also a factor of artefact movement. Because of erosion, a significant part of the soil has been removed from its original location. Recent studies of erosion suggest how a combination of fluvial events - rainsplash, rilling and gully formation - can effect the distribution and visibility of ploughsoil assemblages (Taylor 2000). According to Taylor, 'erosion of fine soil particles by sweethwash and small rills are frequent and regular events on terraced soils and seem unlikely to result in significant downslope movement of artefacts. Instead the regular removal of the silt and fine sand fractions results in an overall loss of soil depth on hillcrests and increase in depth at the bottom of slopes. These changes in soil volume will effect sherd concentrations in the matrix accordingly and thus numbers visible on the surface' (Taylor 2000: 24). Evans and O'Connor argue that 'successive periods of sedentation and human occupation create zones of difference between life and the archaeological record, with greater surface diversity of sites and artefacts on eroding slopes where they are conflated in thin soils, than on valley floors, where they are spaced out by sedimentation' (1999: 89).

Stone is the heaviest material and it is not transported as easily as pottery. Allen observed that after four years, over 60 flints, which represented 80% of the total assemblage, had moved 50 m down-slope (Allen 1991). This indicates that down-slope movement is possible over large distances.

When we look at Eastern Thrace, as I mentioned above, in the Kavaklı-Ortakçı area, the Chalcolithic (Pre-Cucuteni / Maritsa (= Kocatepe) and Karanovo VI) off-site artefacts were found immediately outside of the settlements, which were probably related to ancient land-use. Wilkinson (1982) and Gaffney and Tingle (1989) have interpreted off-site artefacts as resulting from ancient manuring practice. In non-tell sites, arable and grazing land lies in the immediate vicinity of the houses (Chapman 1989: 38). The artefacts were spread to the fields by transporting manure from their residential area. Most of the Chalcolithic off-site finds were sherds and they were very small in size. Only 11 flint implements were found. Some off-site artefacts may also be explained by social or ceremonial activities around the settlements or miscellaneous breakages. Two single-period Chalcolithic settlements are close to each other and, in both, the core of the settlements lies on a slight rise. However, in height of 1 m would not have produced much cumulative artefact movement. On the other hand, some of the off-site artefacts may have been displaced by ploughing or washing down from this slight rise by heavy rain.

The EBA I artefacts on the East side of the Çiftlik stream may be interpreted as a farm or a seasonal field structure. Two small pieces of daub were also collected. The off-site artefacts of EBA II were found mainly to the south-west of the main settlement. The density of the EBA pottery ranges between 0.6 to 1.0 sherds per 100 square meters. In the east, we did not recognize any off-site artefacts. When we interpreted off-site artefacts as resulting from the deposition of refuse in one place, we have not found any artefacts except scrappy sherds. There was only one flint implement. One to four EBA II off-site artefacts were found per "mini-transect" in the south-west area. The interpretation of off-site artefacts as resulting from ancient manuring practice, rises the issue of land holding. Why did the EBA II settlers not use the eastern land for agricultural purposes?

The bed of the Süloğlu Stream is very narrow, constituting a flood-plain ca. 450-500 m wide on both sides. The flood plain of Süloğlu Stream is very fertile and we suppose that the flood-plain was used for agricultural purposes during the prehistoric period. However, in the Tepeyanı-Bağlariçi area, we do not recognize any Chalcolithic off-site artefacts on the flood-plain. The absence of off-site artefacts in the flood-plain may be explained in two ways. First, alluvium is carried by the Süloğlu stream every year and alluvial deposits probably covered the flood-plain. Second, the flood-plains, in general, are fertile areas that need no manuring. On the other hand, the existence and intensity of manuring activities in Neolithic and Chalcolithic periods are still open issues.

Although the Chalcolithic site of Tepeyanı is small, the artefact density is very high. When we compare on-site and off-site densities, off-site density is notably low. There are minor off-site artefact concentrations of Pre-Cucuteni / Maritsa (= Kocatepe) artefacts; two on the low terrace and near the main road, one on the high terrace, ca 500 m far from the settlement and other is located on lower terrace to the North, ca. 300 m far from the settlement. Small off-site concentrations may be explained by seasonal use field huts. Two small concentrations near the main road may also be explained by artificial secondary concentrations near the road, as a result of road construction.

A broken axe was found ca. 150 m far from the settlement. The axe was broken longitudinally, so that reuse was impossible. Probably the axe was broken during tree-felling activities and left on the ground. An ethnographic study shows that, during tree-felling activities among Australian Aborigines, stone tools were left on the ground (Gould 1968).

Summary and Conclusion

Documentation of off-site artefacts is very significant in the study of settlement patterns and land use. In the Edirne region of Eastern Thrace, a block survey in the Kavaklı-Ortakçı area, transect survey in the Tepeyanı-Bağlariçi area and intra site gridded survey have provided important evidence relating to past land use and settlement systems. As a result of our surveys, we propose that most of the settlements in the Edirne region can be described as mobile, re-occupied flat settlements. Settlements in the Edirne region are marked by shifting over a long period. Settlement movement is either dispersed over a small area such as a circle of 1 km radius (e.g. Kavaklı-Ortakçı area), or over wider areas such as a circle of 10-20 km radius (e.g. the Tunca valley). Systematic field collection in the Edirne region shows that only Roman pottery scatters in Eastern Thrace formed an almost unbroken carpet throughout the landscape. Most of the prehistoric off-site artefacts in the Kavaklı-Ortakçı area were found immediately around the settlements and in the Tepeyanı-Bağlariçi area were found in small concentrations around the settlements. The off-site artefacts in the Edirne region may be explained by manuring - probably only in the Early Bronze Age -, seasonal huts or accidental breakage.

I-II SETTLEMENT MOBILITY

Occupation at the settlements of the lower and upper Ergene Basin of Eastern Thrace was marked by a series of abandonments and re-occupations. Settlements can be described as mobile, re-occupied flat settlements. Mobility is a property of individuals, who may move in many different ways, alone or in groups, frequently or infrequently, over long or short distances. Our criterion for defining settlement mobility in the prehistoric settlements of Eastern Thrace is movements of a group from one location to another, with the aim of settling down for a longer or shorter period of time.

The term mobility or mobile societies is generally used for hunter-gatherers (Binford 1980; 1983; Kelly 1992; Foley 1981a). Binford began to unpack the concept of mobility by differentiating between "residential mobility", movements of the entire band or local group from one camp to another, and "logistical mobility", hunter-gatherer movement of individuals or small task groups out from and back to the residential camp (Binford 1980). Binford used these terms for two ideal hunter-gatherer settlement systems - collectors and foragers. Collectors move residentially to key locations and use long logistical forays to bring resources to camp. Foragers 'map onto' a region's resource locations. Foragers do not store food. They make frequent residential moves and short logistical forays. Collectors store food and they make infrequent residential moves but long logistical forays (Binford 1980). Binford later added another term, known as "territorial or long-term mobility" (Binford 1983). A territorially restricted group visits the same places repeatedly each season, using fixed facilities such as shelters. On the other hand, the recent work of Whittle (2001) considered that mobility is not only for hunter-gatherer societies but even for more sedentary social groups.

Planned tell settlements with developed houses and a large quantity of artefacts of the Balkans have generally been accepted as evidence for long-term permanent habitation. However, the concept of long-term permanent occupation has come under criticism due to a re-examination of tell settlements, studies of hunter-gatherer complexity and recent research on the relations between settlements and their landscapes. The study of sedentism in non-Neolithic and Early Neolithic societies and social anthropological studies of complex hunter-gatherers indicate that sedentary life style cannot be used as a hallmark of the Neolithic. If such forms of sedentary life are used as signifiers of especially the earliest Neolithic, then Neolithic society began developing in the Mesolithic. The study of Late Mesolithic and Early Neolithic groups of the Iron Gate suggested that the Iron Gate communities lived in permanent houses, subsistence without dependence on agriculture and animal breeding (e.g. Borić 2002).

A large number of burials have been recorded within the nine Mesolithic sites of the Iron Gates, such as Lepenski Vir, Vlasac, Padina, Schela Cladovei (Radovanović 1996:161). Important work on the hunter-gatherer social complexity in Denmark-Ertebølle Culture, suggested that some of the sites, such as Skateholm I, were seasonal camp sites but buried their dead in a cemetery (Rowley-Conwy 1998). The seasonal occupation of Skateholm I was very large and the adjacent cemetery contains some 50 inhumations. In Oleneostrovski Mogilnik (Red Deer Island) in Karelia, Russia about 177 Mesolithic burials were excavated and the total number of graves at the site has been estimated at more than 400 (O'Shea and Zvelebil 1984; Jacobs 1995). In the other areas of the northern and Western Europe, Mesolithic cemeteries associated with semi-sedentary and / or semi-nomadic (?) groups were also found e.g. Moita do Sebastiao (Roche 1989), Amoreiras (Arnaud 1989) in Portugal and Vedbæk in Denmark (Price 1985), Zvejnicki in Lithuania (O'Shea and Zvelebil 1984), Téviec and Hoëdic in France (Schulting 1996). One might suggest that the cemeteries could be a very important key factor for some hunter-gatherer occupations. Some hunter-gatherer communities occupy fixed settlements at different seasons (cf. territorial mobility of Binford), and these fixed settlements are marked by cemeteries. Tuan correctly argues that the power of symbols in places is dependant upon the depth of the human emotions expected in the fields of care (Tuan 1977). Thus, ancestors probably play one of the important roles for sedentism. On the basis of ethnographical studies, Kent argues that some groups make seasonal trips but return to a permanent camp where they reside for the majority of the year (Kent 1989:2). In Dragsholm in Zedland, Denmark a Mesolithic and a Neolithic grave were found side by side (Bradley 1998:22). A Neolithic cemetery was also preserved on Red Deer Island (Jacobs 1995:347). In the Early Neolithic, burials were found in many sites in Central and Southeast Europe (Borić 1999: Fig.24). However, Early Neolithic burials are small in number compared to Mesolithic burials. Parts of human skeletons were found buried in some important Early Neolithic tells, such as Anza (Némeskeri and Lengyel 1976: 376) Nea Nikomedia and Azmak (Whittle 1996: 59).

We should consider that the broader elements of Neolithic ideology such as the cult of the ancestors or permanent houses can be found already in the Mesolithic. The more established social anthropological studies of complex hunter gatherers also showed that non-sedentary complex communities engaged in activities, ideologies and belief systems little different from those of settled communities (Bradley 1998). Zvelebil argued that there seems to be a considerable continuity in social organisation across the economically defined Mesolithic-Neolithic transition (Zvelebil 1998:23).

Farming societies in the Balkans show sign of mobility. Recent archaeo-geological research in Northern Greece showed that the early agricultural tells in the flood-plain was temporary and not permanent (van Andel et. al. 1995). The research suggests that flood plain tells, such as Platia Magoula Zarkou and Koutsaki Magoula were occupied only outside the flood season. Study of the soil history shows that Early Neolithic activity at both sites occurred when flooding was frequent. Runnels and van Andel noted that many early farming flood plain sites exist in Southeast Europe, for example the Körös settlements in Hungary (van Andel and Runnels 1995: 494). However, more recent investigations in the Tisza region in Hungary showed that only a few Neolithic sites lie on lower elevation on the flood-plain. Most of the sites were set back from the flood-plain edge (Chapman 1994: 81). Wilkie and Savina suggested that the Early Neolithic sites in the Grevena region, South-East Macedonia, do not show the preference for flood-plain environments which van Andel and Runnels suggested for the Larisa basin (Wilkie and Savina 1997). At Anza in Macedonia, no break is known between the early agricultural layers (Gimbutas 1976: 29). Phase I at Anza is the earliest occupation and it is divided into two; Ia and Ib. The transition from Ia and Ib is gradual with no obvious break. Similarly, the cultural sequence at tell of Achilleion, Thessaly, was divided into four main phases, covering without interruption most of the Early and Middle Neolithic (Gimbutas et al. 1989). Bailey suggests that tell settlements in the Balkans such as Ovcharovo in Northeastern Bulgaria are marked by a long series of abandonments and re-occupations (Bailey 1997). According to Bailey, the stratigraphy of Ovcharovo is marked by thirteen episodes of house building and house destruction and collapse (Bailey 1990; 1997). The thirteen horizons documented long-term episodes of settlement abandonment. According to Bailey, the most important evidence for tell abandonment in the North Bulgarian tells is seasonal flooding (Bailey 1997). The specifics of house rebuilding and repair and the use of so-called fortification walls as barriers were attempts to control flooding. However, of the 10 tells investigated by Todorova in Northeast Bulgaria, all are higher than the river by 2 m or more, and only one of them can be described as a flood-plain tell (personal communication, J. Chapman). It seems that, in Southeast Europe, two types of Early Neolithic tell settlements may be recognized; seasonal tells (e.g. Platia Magoula Zarkou) and permanent tells (e.g. Anza).

Another factor in settlement mobility is the transhumant grazing requirements of the settlement's sheep, goat and cattle. Summer conditions in the flood-plains did not favour animal production and people would have taken herds of animals into the neighbouring foothills and highland pastures for grazing (Whittle 1997:20). Whittle argues that (2001) moving from one place to another need not be determined by economic considerations, though they can influence such choices. There are also social and ritual reasons for settlement mobility. For example, Sedentary Tswana settlements in Botswana were traditionally moved every 10 to 15 years (Kent 1989). The death of the household or group leader may also lead to the abandonment (Rivière 1995).

Prehistoric settlements in the Edirne region are marked by shifting over a long period. As a result of surface survey of the Edirne region, two models can be introduced for settlement mobility. I have called the first; "Extensive Mobility". This model may explain the series of abandonments and re-occupation dispersed over one widespread landscape unit or community area such as a permanent stream, highland, coastline etc. The second model is "Restricted Mobility", explaining abandonments and re-occupations of settlements dispersed over small landscape units that are almost the same as those in the Extensive mobility. The size range of "Extensive Mobility" is larger than of "Restricted Mobility". In "Restricted Mobility", the dispersed of settlements has a radius of no more than 1 km. However, in "Extensive Mobility" settlements are dispersed within a radius of 10-20 km in one community area (*Fig. II.1*). Before testing our models, I shall describe the settlement types in Eastern Thrace.

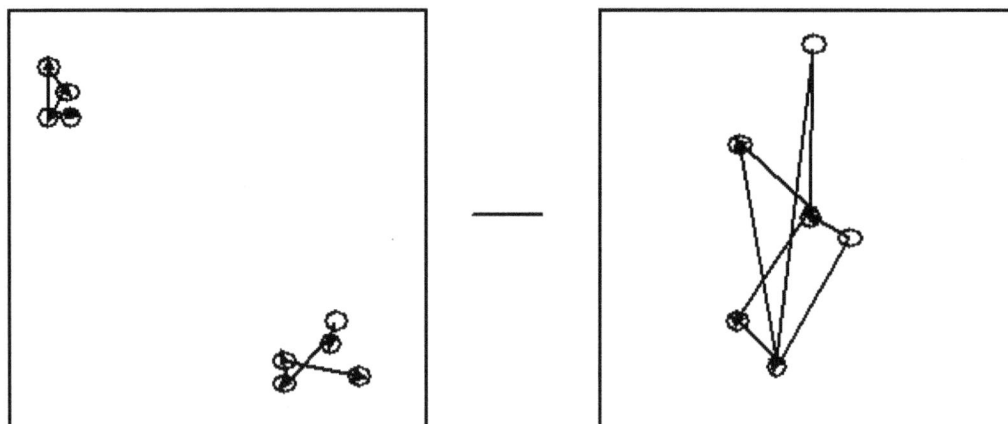

Fig. II.1. Schematic Models of "Restricted" mobility (left) and "Extensive" mobility (right)

Settlement Types of Eastern Thrace

In the Prehistoric Turkish Thrace, two main types of site can be recognised: tells and flat settlements. On the basis of Southeast European settlements, several differences between the spatial organization of tells and flat settlements were outlined by Chapman (1989: 39); 'different locations for communal activity (focal points outdoors for flat settlements, indoor or off-tell for tells), different potential for settlement expansion (greater for flat settlements, less for tells), a different degree of tolerance of dimensional variability (greater for flat settlements, less for tells), and different attitudes to the maintenance of tradition in the landscape (more stability on tells, less stability on flat settlements)'. One of the clear differentiations between tells and flat sites are size. According to Chapman (1989), the individual small family household was the basic residential unit in the Eastern Balkans. Chapman's observations can also be adapted to Eastern Thrace. Model village sizes can be defined for the tell cultures of the East Balkans, where the minimal village community size of 60-120 people is rarely exceeded. Flat settlements in the Eastern Balkans exhibit far greater variability in form, planning and size than standard, an almost model unit of tells. The size range of flat settlements is larger than that of tells. The large nucleated tells occurred later, in the Copper Age (Chapman 1989). However, in Turkish Thrace, the large nucleated tells occurred in the Bronze Age. Another important point of contrast between tells and flat settlements are the degree of potential for settlement growth and expansion. In nucleated tell settlements, the potential degree of growth and expansion is less than for dispersed flat settlements (Chapman 1989). There are also several differences between settlement components on tells and flat settlement. Residence on tells precludes the incorporation of arable or pasture land on to the tell surface. They achieved land holdings as a complex pattern of scattered holdings and a radiating block form. In flat settlements arable and grazing land lies in immediate vicinity of the houses. The juxtaposition of "house and garden" in a spatial unit is strikingly different from those on tells (Chapman 1989).

Settlements from the lower and upper Ergene Basin of Eastern Thrace are marked by flat settlements rather than tell. Tells are the typical settlement type in the Northern shore of the Sea of Marmara and the Gelibolu Peninsula. Only two tells - Keşan-Mezarlık Tepe and Arpalık Tepe-Ipsala - were found in inner Eastern Thrace, dating mostly to the Early Bronze Age. Most of the tells found on the Northern shores of the Sea of Marmara and the Gelibolu Peninsula are also dated to the Early Bronze Age.

Settlement Mobility in the Prehistoric Settlements of the Edirne Region

The settlements of the Edirne region are often situated on sites previously occupied during the earlier periods. However, later arrivals (?) settled not on the top of the early settlements, but always nearby. This pattern fits our "Restricted Mobility" model. Noteworthy among this model is the Kavaklı-Ortakçı area, some 20 km north-east of Edirne. In the Kavakı-Ortakçı area, the settlement history goes back to the Late Neolithic. Kalojanovec-type of pottery is the earliest find to the south of the gulch. We suggest that, during this period, the settlement was small. A Chalcolithic Pre-Cucuteni / Maritsa (= Kocatepe) settlement was found just south of the village and north of the gulch. A Calcolithic Karanovo VI settlement is located ca.100-150 m Southwest of the Pre-Cucuteni / Maritsa (= Kocatepe) settlement, near the gulch. On the East bank of the Çiftlik stream, a concentration of Early Bronze Age I pottery was found. However, it is not clear whether EBA I material constitute actual occupation or off-site activity. A large Early Bronze Age II settlement was found on the South side of the gulch. There is a hiatus in settlement between the Early Bronze Age II and the Late Bronze Age period. A settlement of the Late Bronze Age-Early Iron Age was found at the confluence of the stream and gulch.

The Restricted mobility model of the Edirne region is comparable to those of Asağı Pınar-Kanlıgeçit, near the town of Kırklareli, around 40 km east of Edirne (Özdoğan et al. 1997:3), and Drama in Southern Bulgaria, some 60 km north-west of Edirne (Lichardus et al. 2000). In Aşağı Pınar-Kanligeçit, the settlement history dates back to the Early Neolithic period. In Aşağı Pınar, Karanovo I-II and Karanovo III and III-IV settlements were found almost side by side. A Chalcolithic (Pre-Cucuteni) settlement was found in the south and east Kanlıgeçit area, about 300 m South-West of Aşağı Pınar, South of the Haydardere stream. The Early Bronze Age settlements were found in the North and South Kanligeçit area, on both sides of the Haydardere stream. A small settlement of the Late Bronze / Early Iron Age was found on Yeşilmeydan hill, about 300 m East of Kanligeçit and 200 m South of Aşağı Pınar.

In the Drama micro-region, settlement history dates back also to the Early Neolithic period. Karanovo II and III settlements were found ca. 1,5 km south-east of Drama, on the south bank of the Kalnica Stream. Karanovo IV settlement moved to the south of Drama, ca. 1,5 km west of the Karanovo II and III settlements. The Late Karanovo IV and Karanovo V and IV settlements were found just east of the Karanovo II and III settlements. Early Bronze Age settlements were found on both Karanovo V-VI and Karanovo IV settlements (Lichardus et al. 2000).

Settlement mobility in the Tunca basin is significantly different, and it can serve as an example of our "Extensive Mobility" model. In the Tunca basin, Middle and Late Neolithic (Karanovo III and III-IV) settlements were found on the lower terrace of the river, some 10-30 m above the flood-plain. At the beginning of the Late Neolithic period, new settlements of Kalojanovec-Çardakaltı assemblage, is marked by a shift from the lower terrace to upper terrace settlement, some 60 m above the flood-plain. There is only one Chalcolithic settlement in the area and is located around the Lake of Göl Baba. During the Early Bronze Age, the settlements were situated on the lower and upper river terraces. An Early Bronze Age settlement was also found around the Lake of Göl Baba. With the exception of one site - Kaldırım - the settlements occupied during the earlier phases were not settled during the Early Bronze Age.

Summary and Conclusion

A study of settlement types and mobility in the Eastern Thrace is outlined above. As a result of our surveys, we propose that the prehistoric settlements of the Ergene basin can be described as mobile, re-occupied flat settlements. Settlement movement is either dispersed over a small area such as 1 km radius (Restricted Mobility), or over wider areas such as 10-20 km radius (Extensive Mobility). So far, there are no geomorphological studies, no detailed soil analyses and no pollen diagrams[1] for Eastern Thrace. Hence, for the time being we can only speculate on the factors that contributed to settlement change in Eastern Thrace. It is not yet clear whether settlement change in the region was due to changes in landscape (soils or natural water sources), climate or social factors.

---

[1] In summer 2002 sediment cores were obtained from two locations at the northestern part of the Göl Baba Lake, north of Edirne (Magyari *et al.* 2003). In the near feature we will be able to have the first pollen diagram of Eastern Thrace.

I-III SETTLEMENT TERRITORIES

Analysis of settlement territories appeared as early as the 1970s, when Hodder and Orton (1976) articulated archaeological information using the methods of locational geography. Somewhat earlier, the Cambridge palaeoeconomy group had defined a methodological project on the relationship of settlements to their surrounding in the conceptualisation of site catchment analysis. The site catchment approach was introduced to archaeology by Vita-Finzi and Higgs (1970: 5). They defined the objective as 'the study of the relationships between technology and those natural resources lying within the economic range of individual sites'. The aim is to estimate a site's resource base and overall productivity, is calculated based on a hypothesised economic range (Roper 1979: 120). Throughout the 1970s, many archaeologists adopted the technique widely. However, during the 1980s and 1990s, only limited publications have appeared. The reasons are varied, but can broadly be ascribed to philosophical and technical difficulties. Recently this method was re-investigated by Bintliff (1999). Using ethnographic data, it was estimated that hunter-gatherers normally exploit an area of ca. 10 km radius around their base, or a radius of 2 hour's walk. On the other hand, farming communities, normally use an area of about 5 km radius, or 1 hour's walk (Flannery 1976: 91). The Cambridge palaeoeconomy group suggested that a global average of human walking-time of some 5 km an hour would allow archaeologists to set a territorial radius for sites in each of the three main economies - hunter-gatherer, pastoral and farmer – of 2 hours, 1.5 hour and 1 hour distance respectively from the settlement (Bintliff 1999). In practice, practitioners of catchment analysis had realized that map distance for walking-times of 2, 1.5 and 1 hour varied according to physical relief. On a completely flat plain without a major river crossing, one might walk as much as 7 km in an hour, whereas in a very rugged hill country, one might walk as little as 2 to 3 km an hour as the crow flies away from the settlement (Bintliff 1999). The catchment analysis plots the distribution of varying land classes, topographic details, vegetation and water resources within the territory. According to Bintliff (1999: 507), 'the overall bounded territory was especially favourable for the needs of that past community, but a further consideration of the underlying principle of the friction of distance would suggest that, even with the territory, those resources to be given most attention or demanding most labour would be found closest to the home base. Thus it was predicted that the evaluated contents of the bounded territory would be found to be unusually rich - those resources exploited by the past community compared with their distribution in the region as a whole'. Furthermore, the ancient settlement might have been surrounded by a series of land use zones, up to the territorial boundary, all concentrated around the residential focus, with those subsistence activities demanding most labour being practised in the innermost zones, and the least demanding economic activities being carried out in the outher zones (Bintliff 1999).

There are a number of problems with using catchment analysis. For instance, how we do approximate catchment size and shape with anything but time of distance contours when the site sample is non-systematic? (Roper 1979). Attempts to circumvent these problems have included the approach used by Flannery in his study in Oaxaca, Mexico (1976: 103). His work suggests a zonation of resource use, but also documents a total catchment area far larger than the analytic territory used in most studies. Flannery reversed the procedure, starting with data on the plant, animal, and mineral resources found at sites and asked from how far away must they have come from? The analysis considered all kinds of resources from the commonest plants to the most exotic trade items. It required good faunal and floral preservation, detailed study of those remains, and comprehensive knowledge of resource distributions. Most basic plant and mineral needs were satisfied within 5 km of the site, but animals, wood, and exotic materials came from further away. Bintliff (1999: 522) suggested a simple technique such as Thiessen Polygon rather than taking a measure such an inter-site distance as a reliable guide to the average radius or radius-equivalent of a settlement's catchment. Villages may appear to cluster closely when they are located on a restricted area where resources are clustered. But their individual territories may extend asymmetrically to greater distances. In contrast, in a landscape where resources vary little two-dimensionally or are found widely or discretely, settlement locations may be found to approximate closer to the geometric focus of circular territories. Another important study is that of Foley (1977). He developed an ecological model accounting for differential productivity in an area. This model is free of specific loci instead it uses quadrates superimposed on a general resource zone map where sites are assumed to be located. This approach would then analyse the energy balance by subtracting the value of the energy necessary to exploit an area from a given locus from the extracted energy.

A fundamental criticism using catchment analysis to reconstruct past economic patterns is the assumption that modern resource distributions are similar to those in past times. Changes in climate and environments and their effects on biological and other resources, may present non-measurable distorting factors that are not always taken into consideration. Another criticism of territorial analysis takes issue with the central assumption that past human communities have adapted their behaviour to ecological principles, either intuitively or consciously. For example, ethnographical evidence shows that a village site in Africa is surrounded by an extensive zone of the poorest agricultural land, beyond which lies far better soil. The reason for this situation was prolonged, intense, cultivation of the area closest to these villages in a landscape with naturally poorly developed soils, resulting in soil impoverishment. This society practiced a cyclical relocation of villages onto fresh soils when land exhaustion reached a critical level, in a pattern of shifting agriculture (Bintliff 1999). The Nuba of the Sudan, whose farming villages lie along very poorly resourced ridges, avoiding fertile valley land below. The reason was the valley land has become occupied by a different ethnic group that has driven the indigenous people into marginal hill locations for their livelihood (Bintliff 1999).

Here, it is time to talk about the concept of community area outlined by Neústupný (1991) in the study of prehistoric settlement patterns. In this formulation, the landscape was divided into more or less regular spatial segments corresponding to basic economic and social units, that is, to prehistoric communities. The presupposition of the segmented character of the cultural landscape is based upon theoretical generalization about the prehistoric economy and social system. The concept of community areas is based upon the notion of a community sharing a common territory and co-operating in certain economic and social activities. The community areas were divided using the method of Thiessen polygons, each focused on either single or multiple sizes of sites. Each community area has a certain function that corresponds to the practical needs of the community that settled it (Neústupný 1998). Thiessen polygons was used to identify potential territorial boundaries. The resulting polygon is considered to bind the areas that would have been most efficiently served by settlements, for every point within the polygon is closer to its central place than to any other. The polygons are created by drawing straight lines between each contemporary pair of neighbouring sites, then at the mid-point along each of these lines a second series of lines, at right angles to the first are drawn. Linking up the second series of lines creates the Thiessen polygons, and in this way a whole area can be apportioned among the sites it contains (Hodder and Orton 1976: 60).

Settlement Territories and Past Economic Organization in the Prehistoric Settlements of the Edirne region

The Early Chalcolithic and the Early Bronze Age settlements in the Edirne region may allow us to analyse settlement territories. First of all, I can say that it is difficult to identify precise hierarchical relationships between settlements in the Edirne Region. However, the size of Early Chalcolithic, Pre-Cucuteni / Maritsa (= Kocatepe) settlements indicate that there are small settlements associated with large settlements. Flannery's catchment analysis may be used for Kavaklı 2. Kavaklı 2 is the largest Late Chalcolithic (Pre-Cucuteni / Maritsa) site in the Edirne

Region. It is located in an area at the edge of the Istranca Mountains. The Istranca Mountain contains copper, rock and wood sources and serves as a highland pastures for grazing. Kavaklı 2 needed about 2.5 km radius or a half-hour walk to satisfy the entire basic agricultural requirement. On the other hand, a catchment of more than 5 km radius, or one hour's walk, was required to satisfy the mineral resources requirements and also to provide highland pastures for grazing. A small flint source was available more than 5 km to the south and sources of rock (mainly gneiss) and a clay for making pottery was also available within 5 km radius (*Fig. III.1*).

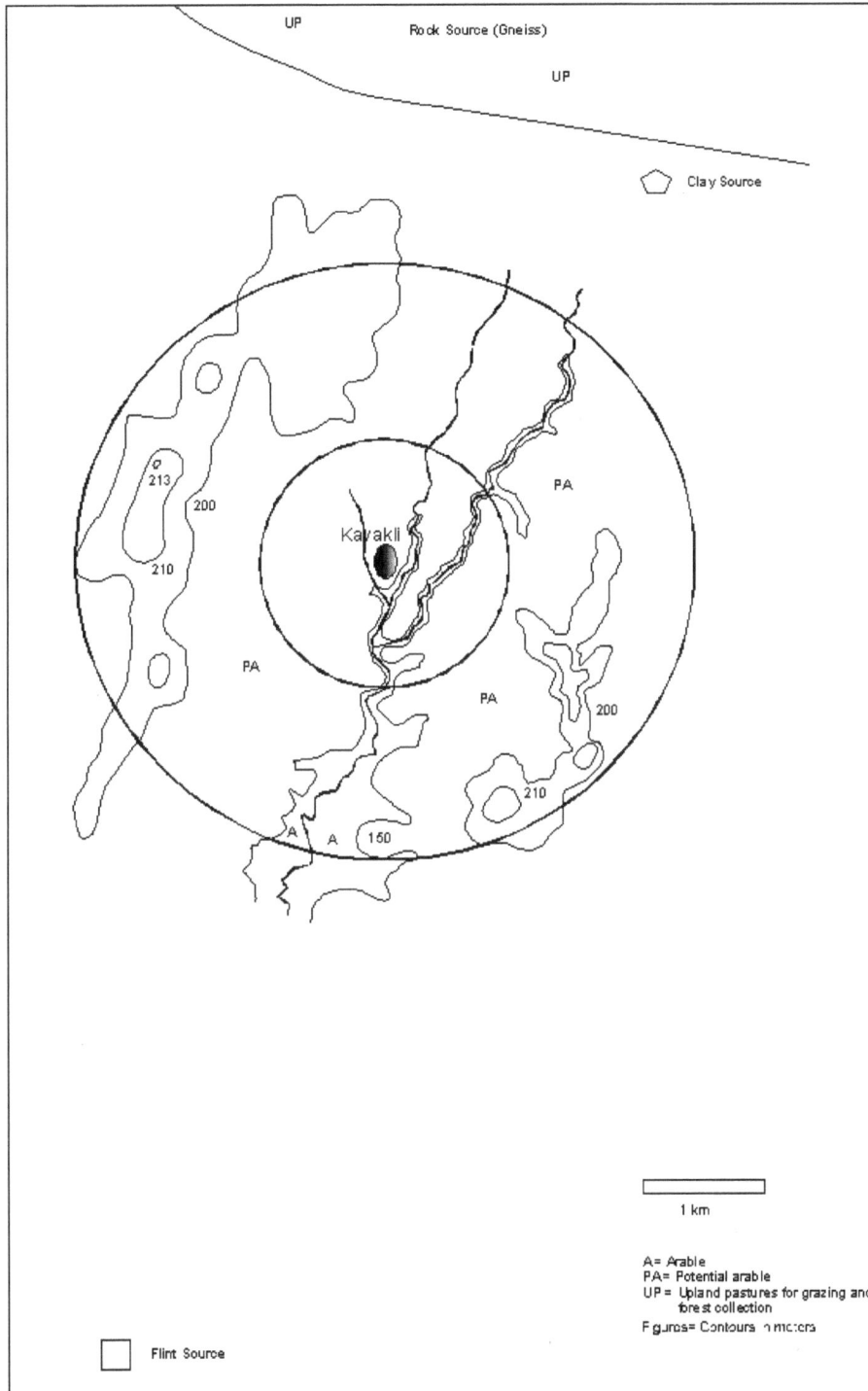

Fig. III.1. The catchment and exploitation territory of Kavakli 2

The small Pre-Cucuteni / Maritsa (= Kocatepe) settlements are situated on stream terraces to the south. These settings would have provided access to fertile flood-plain soils, suitable for agriculture. They are located on linear streams. It seems that streams in the South are colonized by daughter settlements. They needed less than 2.5 km radius or half-hour walk to satisfy all of the basic agricultural requirements and to include some seasonal plants in the upland. We assume that colonisation of the streams with daughter settlements should be economic. There was probably a hierarchy between the small and large settlements. The small settlements may supply agricultural products to the big settlements, and the big settlements may supply them products such as flint and copper.

In the Edirne region, it seems that during the Early Bronze Age there were large centres acting as the cores of community areas. Flannery's work about determination of site catchments and territory analysis can be applicable in the Early Bronze Age settlements in the Tunca Valley. In the Tunca Valley, Early Bronze Age settlements were constrained by the linear character of the river. Three Early Bronze Age settlements - Düştübakyaması, Kaldırım and Çardaklı - were all found on the western bank of the river. Düştübakyaması is the largest settlement, about 75.000 sq. meters in size. It is situated on a high terrace, commanding fairly extensive cultivable lands. Kaldırım and Çardaklı are situated on lower river terraces, and are ca. 40-50.000 sq. meters in size. An Early Bronze Age settlement was also found in the eastern side of the Göl Baba Lake, ca 1.5 km east of the Tunca River. It is also ca 40-50.000 sq. meters in size. The question is how much territory is required to feed the estimated population of the three settlements. It seems that Çardaklı, Kaldırım and Göl Baba were small hamlets of less than a 100 people, and they needed a small area of alluvial land. It is assumed that each settlement used an area of 2.5 km radius, or half-hour walk. However, they needed less than 2.5 km radius to satisfy the entire basic agricultural requirement. Düştübakyaması suggest a territory of 5 km radius, or one-hour walk. However it also needed about 2.5 km radius to satisfy the entire basic agricultural requirement. Theoretical territories were created using Thiessen polygons (*Fig. III.2*).

For settlement pattern analysis of the Tunca River, I would like to introduce a new model - the landscape model. There are two important factors for this model. The first is physical relief. As Bintliff suggests, the map distance for walking-times of 2, 1.5 and 1 hour varied according to physical relief. On a completely flat plain without a major river crossing, one might walk as much as 7 km in an hour, whereas in very rugged hill country, one might walk as little as 2 to 3 km. Vegetation is also important. The second factor is topography. We assumed that topographic features such as hills and streams could be borders between settlements. According to Williams, the obvious boundaries are related to prominent land forms such as, hills, mountains, cliffs, streams, rivers and watersheds. Other boundaries may be marked by changes in gradient on a slope on changes in vegetation or soil or rock types (Williams 1982: 141-143). It is not clear, what was the past vegetation along the Tunca River, including the past dynamics of the river. However, when we look at Düstübakyaması, the people living in the settlement need to cross a major river to the east and north, and they need to climb hills of 150-200 m altitude to the west. Only the southern part is a relatively flat plain. To the west of the settlement, hills about 120-130 m runs from north to south parallel to the river. These hills probably constitute the western territories of the settlement. To the east, the Tunca River and the Göl Baba Lake probably constitute the eastern territories of the settlement. Yassitepe (99 m.) in the south probably constitute a border between Düstübakyamasi and Çardakli. The first meander of the river constitutes the northeastern territory of the settlement, and the Kişra Stream probably constitutes the north-western territory of the settlement. Eski Tabya (157 m) is the important topographic feature to the east. It probably constitutes a border between Çardakaltı and Göl Baba. Theoretical territories of settlements created using the landscape model can be seen in *Fig. III.3*. In Addition, as *Fig. III.1* shows the landscape model can perfectly be apply for the Late Chalcolithic settlement of Kavaklı 2.

Summary and Conclusion

It is difficult to identify precise hierarchical relationships between settlements in the Edirne region as well as the whole Eastern Thrace. However, in the Edirne region, it seems that during the Early Bronze Age there were settlements acting as the cores of community areas. Flannery's work about determination of site catchments and territorial analysis can be applicable to the Early Bronze Age settlements in the Tunca Valley. We assumed that the Early Bronze Age settlements of the Tunca River used an area of 2.5 km radius or half-hour walk. Theoretical territories were created using Thiessen polygons. Other method, the landscape method indicates that geographical features such as hills and streams may have acted as boundaries.

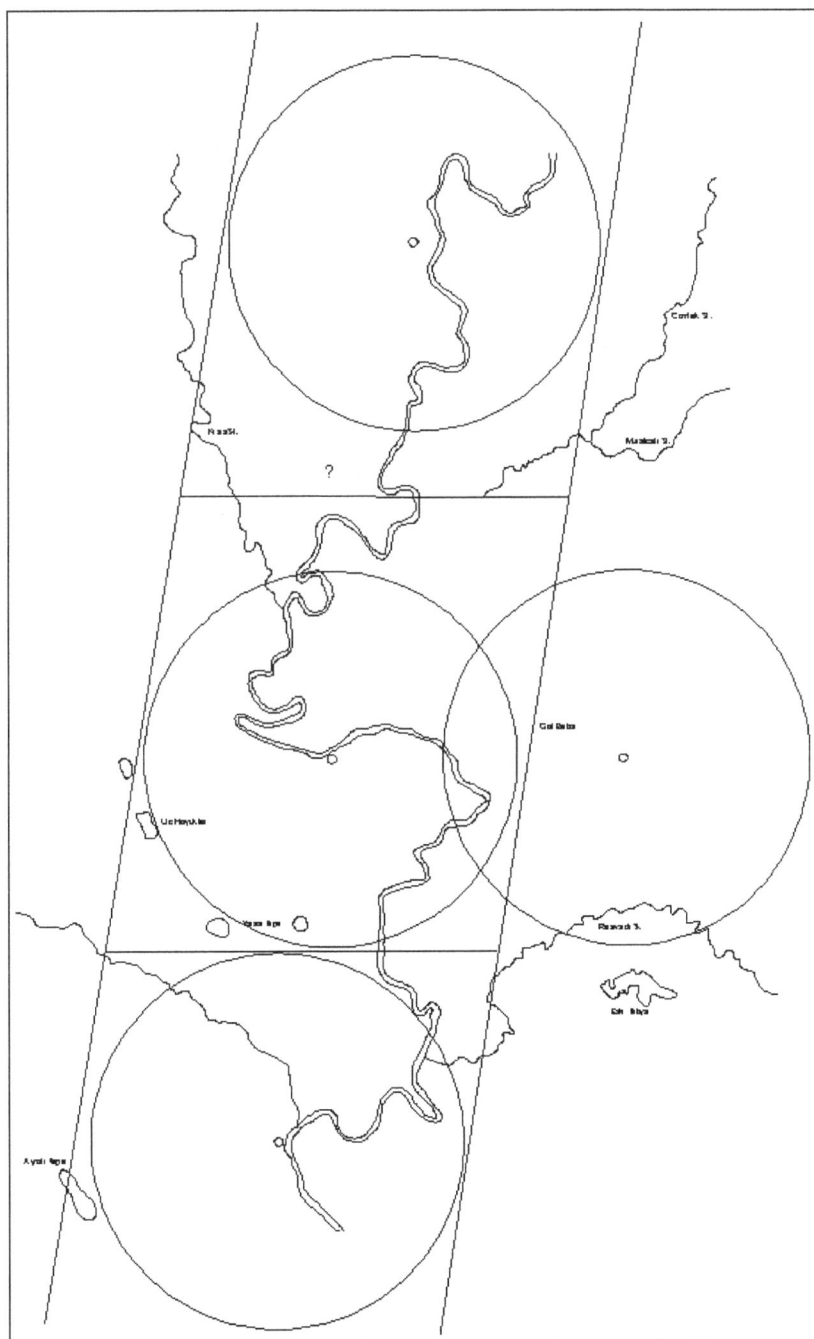

Fig. III.2. EBA settlements in Tunca basin. 2.5 km radius territories modified by use of Thiessen Polygons

39

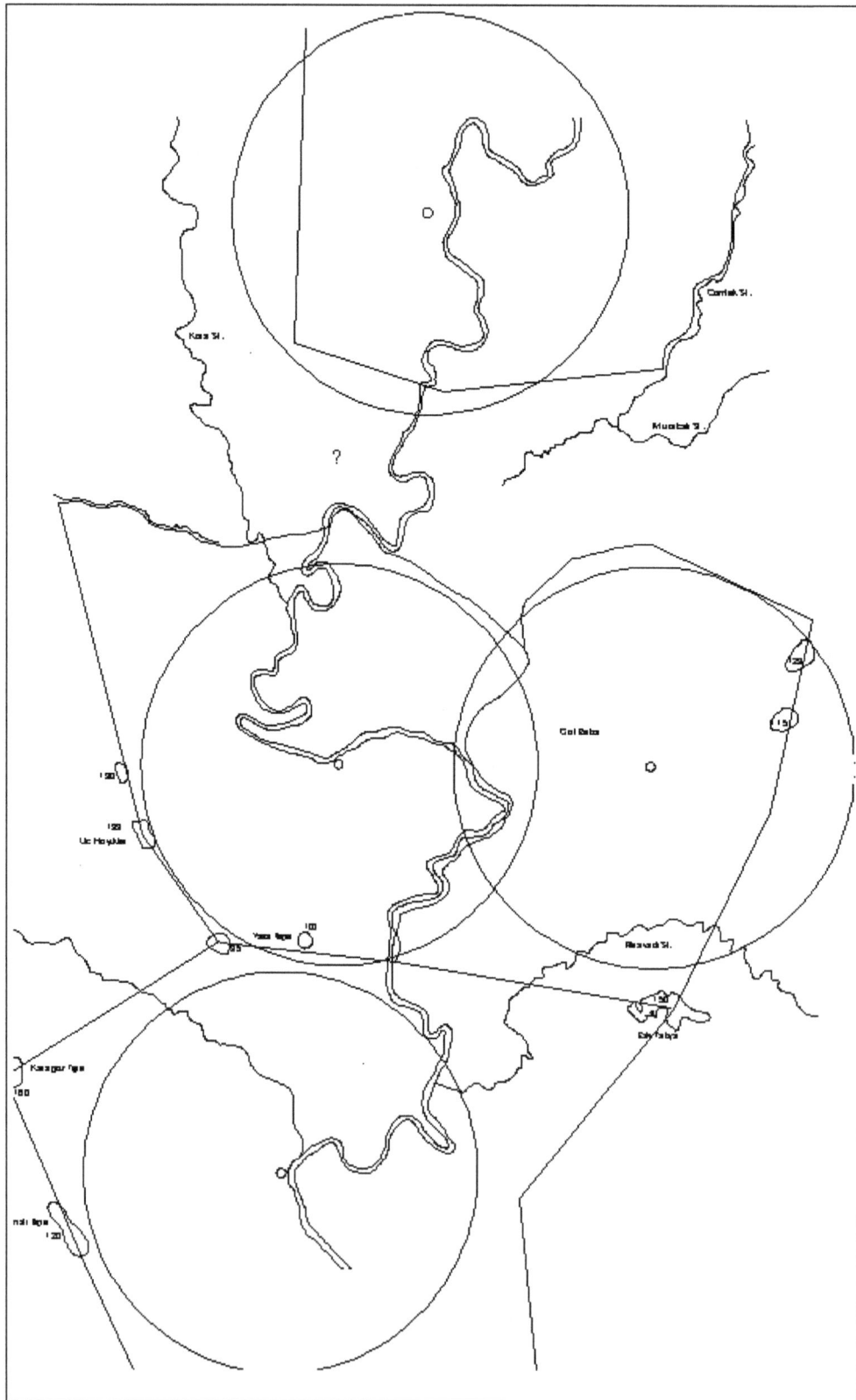

Fig. III.3. EBA settlements in Tunca basin. 2.5 km radius territories modified by using the Landscape model

PART II
READING THE SETTLEMENTS

II-IV STONE AXE PRODUCTION SITES OF EASTERN THRACE

According to R. Wagner (1975:77) 'in learning how to use tools, we are secretly learning how to use ourselves'. He claims that tool use is about the objectification of our skills as controls which tools place on the relationship between humans and the environment. In prehistoric times, stone served as the main material for making tools. Only stones that met certain technological requirements were used and they were deliberately sought out. Stone is most intractable and the most difficult material to work on. Each stone tool took so much labour to produce that it was among the most valued of a person's possessions. The polished stone axe was a very significant tool type during the prehistoric period. The polished stone axe provided a central symbol within prehistoric society because it effectively linked a whole range of spheres of human activity (Tilley 1996: 114). The axe was a basic tool in subsistence, an important exchange item linking together communities, personal status and prestige item in a community. Stone axes circulating within society had a value, which would have been related to debt and kinship, and to the articulation of relationships between persons and groups (Thomas and Tilley 1993: 290). They had a significance, which is functional, and a meaning, which is concerned with the content of ideas and symbols. According to Tilley (1996: 114), 'the axe provided a durable symbolic medium for creating and maintaining social ties and dependencies through ritual and everyday activities'.

K. Kristiansen (1984: 79) has argued that the axe links together agricultural production, exchange, ritual consumption and feasting. Ethnographical studies show that the leader in lineage groups in the Pokou, Ussiai and Matankol people of the Admiralty Islands is in possession of the axe / adze and can also pass it on to his successor (Ohnemus 1998: 152). He holds the axe / adze in his hand while speaking and dancing in ceremony. On a sad occasion, such as a death in the tribe, the leader appears without his axe / adze. The axe / adze is also used in peacemaking talks or punishment. It stands for law and order, peace and joy. Among Australian Aboriginal societies, the stone axe was prominent in several circumstances, such as in interpersonal relations, in the totemic system and in the wider belief system (Taçon 1991:194). Axes have had aesthetic and symbolic value.

Axes probably had important roles in ceremonial activities. In the Papua New Guinea highlands, the largest axes were valued especially for ceremonial and display purposes (White and Modjeska 1978: 29). In the Mt. Hagen area, three major axe types were recognized: ceremonial, bride-price and work axes (Chappell 1987: 77). Ceremonial axes which were deliberately fashioned as objects of beauty. These axes are usually long, thin and finely finished. They were carried on ceremonial occasions and sometimes used in warfare. Bride-price axes are also well grounded and sharpened, but not as well as the ceremonial axes. They were used only as a bride-price payments and death compensation. Work axes were generally smaller and thicker than ceremonial and bride-price axes. They are not well ground. These axes were used for everyday tasks and were carried on ordinary occasions.

During the mortuary feast of the Sabarl Islanders of Papua New Guinea, the dead paternal clan publicly presents five ceremonial axes to its maternal clan heirs. In absolute secrecy, the axes are used to construct an effigy of the corpse of the honoured dead (Battaglia 1983: 291). The axes were put next to the dead against one another with the heads facing in the same direction. The corpse of the axes is made by propping the handles against each other so the axes rest on their blades. They are said to represent a human body reclining in its grave. The axes and the dead become intertwined in the grave. Then, the dead is raised as it were from the grave and re-installed at the centre of reproductive life. This marks the beginning of his life as an ancestor

41

and establishes him as a source of economic and spiritual aid for the living. The corpse is magically endowed with the power to reproduce axe blades; it becomes more than a representation of the ancestor, it becomes a concrete substitute for the "child" as a reproductive unit of his / her society (Battaglia 1983: 298).

Axes may serve as points of reference for broader belief systems. Axes are found in ritual and funerary contexts, particularly in assemblages from megalithic monuments. In Neolithic chamber tombs in Brittany, the deposition of particular types of stone axes is relatively restricted, especially those that had been obtained from great distances (Patton 1991). By passing from hand to hand, over the distance from their sources, each axe would have build up its own genealogy, as myths became attached to them (Kristiansen 1984: 79). The tomb may act to fix all of those myths in one location. Axes were so deeply connected with the person that the history of the axe and the person becomes intertwined. Thus the burial of the axes introduced the presence of this person to the depositional context (Thomas and Tilley 1993: 293). In Neolithic chamber tombs in Brittany, some of the axes were deliberately broken (Thomas and Tilley 1993: 290-291). Axes may be regarded as having biographies, like persons. They are born (produced), exchanged and destroyed (die). As Chapman argued (2000a), the relationship between fragmented objects and persons is an important, interpretative link. Axes were deeply connected with person and when the body dies, the axes were ritually destroyed. The axes from Tumulus-St. Michel were found in a deposit of ashes and burnt bone, and had been placed vertically (Patton 1991: 67). According to Patton (1991: 70), the ritual position of axes in tombs and also the carved representations of axes in tombs referred to a relationship with the ancestors, death and the past.

Gender division of the axe is significant. Among the Australian Aboriginal groups in the Yir Yoront of North Queensland and Western Arnhem Land, stone axes and other tools were recognized as belonging to men, especially older man, and embodied their ancestral power (Taçon 1991: 194-195). The women and young must borrow the axe from the older male. In the borrowing, the status, position and power of older males were reinforced. Aborigines also believed that the axes are formed from ancestral bones.

In the centre of the chamber at Mané-er-Hroëk, Brittany, a large ring of jadeite and a huge axe were arranged so that its butt penetrated the ring. Behind the blade of the axe were two beads and behind this were a perforated axe and a further bead. All these axes and beads are set along a north-south axis. According to Thomas and Tilley (1993: 291-293), the sexual symbolism is here quite explicit that all axes represent phalluses. Thus the axe may in some contexts be seen as a male attribute.

In the Sabarl Island society, the axes are objectified persons and identified with the bodies of the persons making them (Battaglia 1983:295). The axe blade is called "Hinona"; the "content" or "vital substance" of the valuable. In the context of the physical person, "Hinona" is the term for "genitals" and "right hand"; a symbolism associated with economic and biological reproduction. The axe blade broadly represents the reproductive potential of the singular person (Battaglia 1990: 133; Tilley 1999: 73). Witchcraft is said to eat the hinona away. As the term for the genitals "hinona" also refers to reproductive energy. In this manner, "hinona" is a term that provides the metaphorical connection between persons and ceremonial axes (Battaglia 1983: 293).

Prehistoric Axe factories in EasternThrace

Factories or manufacturing areas are places where craft specialists perform a limited set of activities on a frequent, perhaps regular basis in order to produce items for exchange with other group of people. Stone axe factories or manufacturing areas were recently found in Eastern Thrace. In 1989, a large number of roughouts was sold to İstanbul Museum by a farmer from the Şarköy region. Scholars working in Eastern Thrace were looking for a long time for the site from which these roughouts came. In 1995, the stone axe factory of Yartarla was found by M.A. Işin, director of Tekirdağ Museum, and he demonstrated that the roughouts held in İstanbul Museum come from Yartarla[1]. Later, two more axe factories or manufacturing areas - Hamaylıtarla (Buruneren)[2] and Fener Karadutlar - were found by O. Özbek in the Şarköy region. Since intensive archaeological surface surveys have not yet been conducted in the Şarköy region, it is possible that more such sites exist.

The stone axe factory of Yartarla is located ca. 14 km northwest of Şarköy, ca. 3 km northeast of the village of Sofuköy (*Fig. IV.1*). It is situated on a high terrace of the Kavak Suyu River. The Kavak Suyu River rises in the Ganos Mountain, and descends westwards to the Gulf of Saroz. It has a flat, marshy, alluvial mouth. The Kavak Suyu runs through wide gorges, with steep sides that in some places rise vertically from the river, reaching a height of 200-250 m, on which Yartarla was formed. Hamaylıtarla (Buruneren) and Fener Karadutlar are situated on well-watered lowlands at the southern foot of Mount Helvacı and Sarıkayalar (*Fig. IV.1*). Hamaylıtarla (Buruneren) is located ca. 17 km west of Şarköy and ca. 7 km west of the village of Kızılcaterzi. Fener Karadutlar is situated on Cape İnce, on the northern shore of the Sea of Marmara, ca. 7 km southeast of Hamaylıtarla. The southern foot of Mount Helvacı, Kazanağzı stream and a number of small seasonal streams run into the Sea of Marmara, constituting a small flat of fertile cultivated land.

All axe factories were found associated with prehistoric settlements. In all examples, roughouts, flakes and hammerstones were found to spread over a large area (*Fig. IV.2*). Most of roughouts are waste material, which were broken during the production stage. The weight of roughouts varies from 0.4 kg to 1.0 kg (Özbek 2000). The form of the roughouts indicates that two types of axes were produced in the factories - a large, oval, symmetrical axe with a rounded-butt and a thin-butted slender axe. According to Özbek (2000), they should be regarded as an adze / axe rather than a symmetrical axe[3]. Hammerstones are generally spherical. Özbek observed that broken roughouts were transformed into hammerstones (Özbek 2000). The material recovered in the axe factories consisted almost entirely of flakes[4]. The weight of the flakes varies from 0.2 kg to 0.8 kg (Özbek 2000).

Raw material Source and Axe-manufacturing Processes

Petrological analyses show that all the axes are manufactured from the same rock. This rock is identified as metabasite (Özbek and Erol 2001). An example from the stone axe factory of Yartarla was investigated at the University of Durham, Department of Geology by C. H. Emeleus. He believes that it is an altered igneous rock, mostly altered mica, turbid feldspars and quartz. It contains some iron opaque and weakly pleochroic amphibolites (*Fig. IV.3*). He also believes that it might have come from the low-grade metamorphism. 10 examples from Fenerkaradutlar and 5 examples from Hamaylıtarla were also investigated by K. Erol and O. Özbek (Özbek and Erol 2001). They explain :

---

[1] Finds from Yartarla were first published in a popular magazine by M.A. Isın : Isın, M.A., 1999. Şarköy'ün Antik Baltaları. *Atlas* 74:26.

[2] Hamaylıtarla (Buruneren) was first discovered by M. A. Isın in the early 1990s. This site is not the same site that M. Özdoğan published in 1986 (Özdoğan 1986). A stone axe from the same area was also found in the 1930s, and now it is stored in the Museum of Anatolian Civilizations at Ankara (Kurtoğlu 1938). It is reminding the EBA battle-axes.

[3] According to Semenov (1970: 126), an axe is recognized by its symmetrical profile while an adze by its unsymmetrical profile.

[4] Özbek suggests that (2000: 169) flakes are very difficult to notice and the quantity of flakes collected on the site is too small to make a statistical analysis. However, we observed very large quantity of flakes in Hamaylıtarla as well as Yartarla.

«La roche est formée essentiellement par de la trémolite et de l'actionolite (60%). Ces minéraux peuvent être observés dans les roches d'une manière désordonnée; soit dans la forme de porphyroblastes grossiers, soit dans la forme de petit cristaux. Leures formes cristallines aussi varient, de fibres à la forme en bauettes.

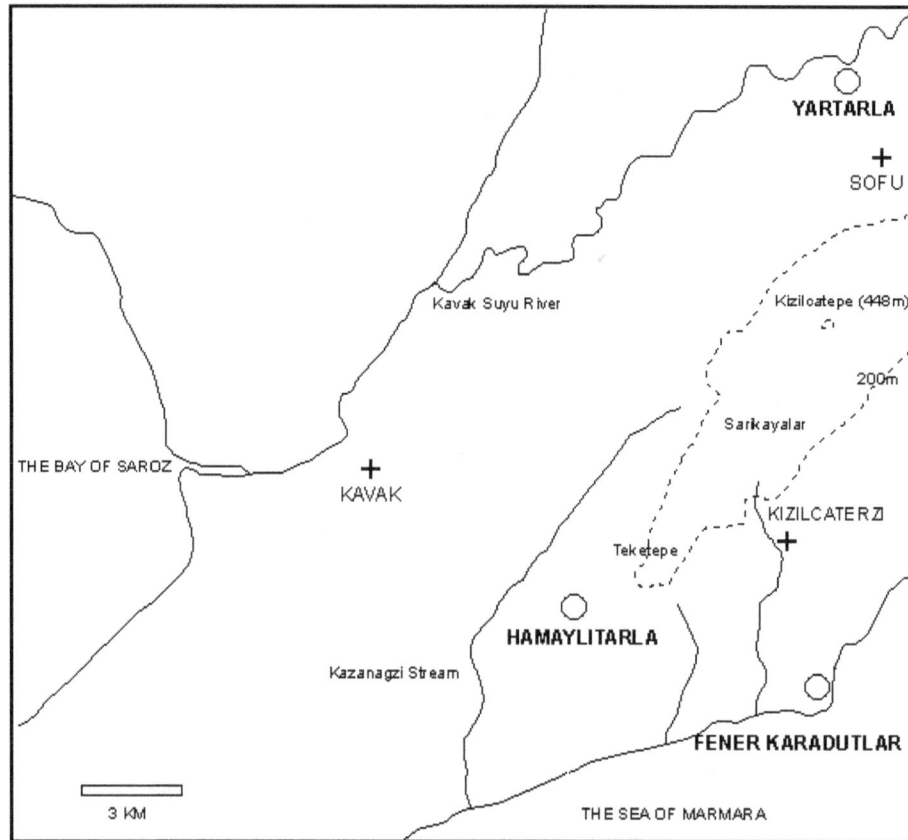

Fig. IV.1. Location map of axe factories in the Şarköy region

Fig. IV.2. An axe working floor at Yartarla.

44

Les plagioclases forment 30 % de la roche. Ils sont fortement transformés en séricite et en mineraux argileux. Titanite, épidote et des mineraux opagues sont des minéraux accessoires. Le quartz est aussi largement présent comme minéral secondaire remplissant les vides et les fractures.» (Özbek and Erol 2001: 5).

The source of the rock is the western outcrops of the Ganos Mountain. The Ganos Mountain extends from northeast to southwest, with steep towards the Sea of Marmara. Its highest point is at Ikizcebaşı with an elevation of about 702 meters. The source used for stone axes occupies the western part. The rock can be obtained as boulders from many different parts of the western outcrops of Ganos Mountain. It always seems to have been assumed that there are two types of quarries for localizing stone. In the first case, rocks outcropping on the surface are reduced to flakes and cores by block-on-block percussion techniques (Torrence 1986: 51). At the second type of quarry, the desired raw material outcrops below the surface and it is therefore necessary to dig pits to extract it. According to Özbek, only the first case applies for the Sarköy factories (personal communication). A general understanding of manufacture is the "chaîne opératoires", which define a number of stages of production as I mentioned above. Ethnographical studies among the Australian Aboriginal groups and the tribes of Indonesia and Papua New Guinea highlands gave important information about axe-manufacturing processes (Blackwood 1950; Dickson 1981; Pétrequin and Pétrequin 1994; Pétrequin *et al.* 1998; Hampton 1999). Seven technological steps are followed by Unda and Kimyal people of Irian Jaya, Indonesia: 1. Locate a suitable boulder core. 2. Break the boulder core. 3. Reduce large pieces to manageable sizes. 4. Shape preform bifaces. 5. Dull edges and grind platforms. 6. Detail fine-flaking. 7. Grind finely flaked bifaces to finished adze blades (Hampton 1999: 257). For procedure 4, each toolmaker used two or three hammerstones. Parallel or longitudinal removals are more favoured (Pétrequin *et al.* 1998: 287). Grinding processes occur near water. Sometimes toolmakers set their grinding stones by the front of their houses and add water (Hampton 1999:272; Blackwood 1950:15). The specific knowledge possessed by axe makers enabled the manufacture of axes.

Axe-manufacturing processes in axe factories in Eastern Thrace were investigated by O. Özbek (2000). He has observed an intensive practice of knapping and pecking. The rock is obtained from the source as boulders and knapping takes place with the help of a hammer stone until a "pre-form" is achived. Again, using a hammerstone the definitive shape is obtained by pecking. This "pre-axe" form has a definitive shape but the tool still has a rough surface. The raw material is very hard and difficult to work on. It is impossible to polish right after knapping. In many examples, whole surface of axes were intensively pecked. Finally, the piece is polished and the blade is sharpened. It seems always to have been assumed that production of roughouts usually took place near the source of raw materials, with the final polishing and sharpening occurring on settlements.

On the basis of ethnographical studies in Irian Jaya, Indonesia, Pétrequin and others (1998: 287) have constructed a series of models of prehistoric technological complexity. 1. the direct polishing of small, naturally pre-formed blocks; 2. knapping by longitudinal removal on small blocks whose naturally occurring was favourable; 3. knapping by transverse removal on small blocks whose natural occurrence was favourable; 4. the thinning of small blocks by longitudinal and transversal removals; 5. the débitage of longitudinal blades from the edge of a large block, worked as a core. There is no evidence for model 1 in the stone axe factories of Eastern Thrace. However, models 4 and 5 are much more common.

Distribution of Stone Axes

The distribution of goods from sources to people desiring them is an important function of the exchange system. According to Hodder (1982a: 209), 'exchange involves the transfer of items that have symbolic and categorical associations. Within any strategy of legitimation, the

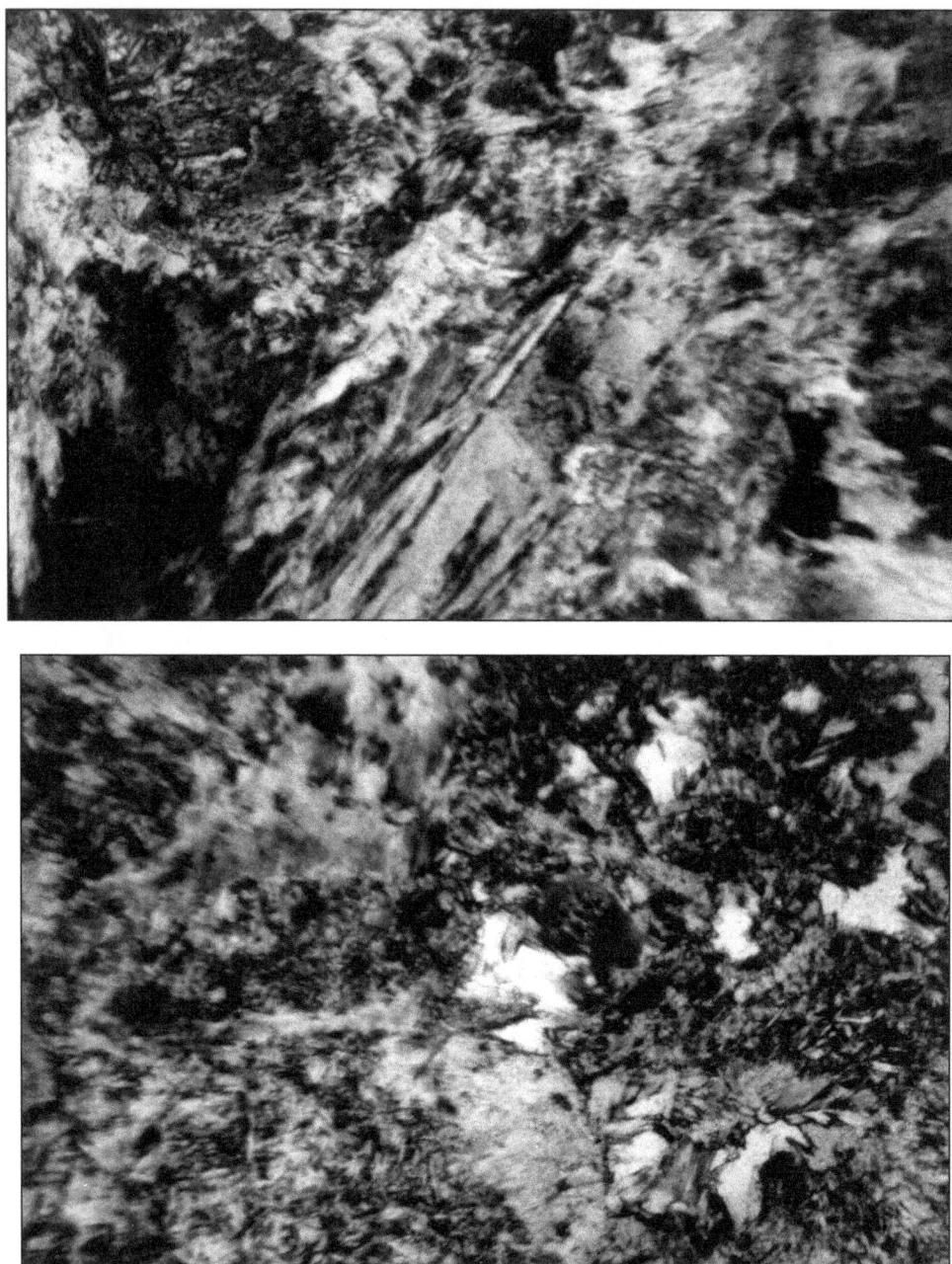

Fig. IV.3. Thin sections of stone axe samples from Yartarla (top) and Yağcılı (bottom)
Polorised light, height of fields 1 mm

symbolism of objects is manipulated in the construction of relations of dominance. The exchange of appropriate items forms social obligations, status and power, but it also legitimates as it forms. A fully contextual approach to exchange must incorporate the symbolism of the objects exchange'. Hodder's idea was influenced significantly by both the pioneering study of Malinowski (1922) in "kula" exchange system of Melanesia, and by the work of Mauss in gift exchange (1925). These ideas were further developed by Sahlins (1972). A gift was a gesture and a bond, imposing obligations on both parties, especially on the recipient. Individual X would establish or reinforce a relationship with individual Y by means of a gift, a value object that would pass from the hands of X to those of Y. The overseas contacts of some islands in Melanesia centred on the ceremonial exchange with their exchange partners within the "kula". "Kula" is an exchange network (Leach and Leach 1983). Exchanges such as these, where the transfer of specific objects as gifts is only one part of relationship with other obligations and with other activities, such as feasting, are said to take place within a framework of reciprocity. Both Mauss and Sahlins recognized that exchange in non-western societies is really a form of diplomacy, and for this reason it cannot be understood in purely "economic" terms. Exchange plays a central role in mediating marriage ties, kinship bonds and alliances, and is crucially important in competition for status. In this sense it is deeply implicated in the classification and circulation of people (Bradley and Edmonds 1993: 12). Exchange also has a strategic role, for giving can be a way of inflicting dept. Every gift presupposes another in return, and lasting differences of social position may result when debtors are unable to discharge their obligations (Gosden 1989). The gift requires future reciprocation, and thus symbolises a lasting obligation over time (Barrett 1989: 308). By passing from one person to another, the exchanged object acquires a history which refers not only to the past and present order of social relations, but also to future ties and obligations. Exchange is thus an important medium through which debts and obligations are built up (Edmonds 1995). Torrence (1986: 5) argued that items might be exchanged as unchanged raw materials, partially modified preforms, or as completed tools. All the separate stages in this very general system - acquisition, production, distribution (exchange) and use - will be interrelated such that behaviour in one sphere partially causes and to some degree is caused by behaviour in another (Torrence 1986: 6).

Clark (1965; 1989: 194) suggests that a system of gift exchange was in operation in the British Neolithic axe trade. Patton (1991: 71) argued that the axe could become a key symbol in an ideological system concerned to stress inter-generational bonds and obligations in relation to ritual practice and the ancestors. According to Bradley and Edmonds, the movement of stone axes cannot be studied in terms of modern economic principles. What we call the axe trade was linked to broader questions of communication and control (Bradley and Edmonds 1993: 205).

In Eastern Thrace, petrological investigations of the stone axes are still in progress. In the Edirne region two examples, one from the Neolithic site of Yağcılı another from the Chalcolithic site of Arpaç have been investigated. The results show that an example from Yağcılı ca. 140 km north of Şarköy, was made of the same rock as the Şarköy region (*Fig. IV.3*). In addition, at the Early Neolithic site of Hoca Çeşme, ca. 85 km east of Şarköy, stone axes were made of the same rock as the Şarköy region (Özbek 2000; Erdoğu 2000).

Dating Prehistoric Axe Factories

Although hundreds of stone axes are being discovered at excavations each year in the Balkans and Anatolia, until now no prehistoric axe factories have been found. However, at the site of Divostin in Serbia, numerous unfinished axe specimens indicate the method of manufacture. In Divostin phase II, a working floor with roughouts, drilling pieces, flakes and also a large pit filled with flakes of roughouts were found (Prinz 1988:257-259 and Plan IIIa). This concentration in Sector B, seems to indicate an area where stone axes were manufactured. Divostin phase II is dated to the Late Vinča Culture. In Obre II in Bosnia, the regular shapes of sixteen stone axes were found between two stone slabs in sounding D, together with two big flint knives, three bone awls and two round baked clay objects. This has been interpreted as an axe-making area (Benac 1973:82 and Fig 13a). A similar axe-making area was also found in sounding VII at Obre II (Benac 1973:82). Obre II, sounding D is dated to the Classic Butmir Culture. However, the dates from sounding VII in Obre II fall earlier. In excavations at Selevac in Serbia, an axe-making area was found outside the House 1, dating ca. 5020-4600 / 4540 cal. BC (Voytek 1990). Recently, an axe making area was found at the Neolithic settlement of Makri in Greek Thrace (personal communication, N. Efstratiou). In Bosnia, at the site of Kalosević-Malo Brdo a large number of flaked stone axe roughouts was discovered (Chapman 1976:146). The pottery on the site was found to date to the Late Vinča Culture. Kalosević-Malo Brdo is probably a prehistoric axe factory; however, there are, as yet, no detailed investigations.

The dating of the axe factories of Eastern Thrace is problematic. There are, as yet, no systematic excavations of axe factories. In the settlement of Yartarla, Late Chalcolithic and Early Bronze Age sherds were collected. The settlement of Fener Karadutlar was completely destroyed by a Byzantine church; only a few Early Bronze Age sherds were found. In the settlements of Hamaylıtarla (Buruneren), Early Neolithic sherds together with a few Early Bronze Age sherds were collected. It seems evident that, without excavations, it is difficult to date these stone axe factories. Petrological investigation of polished stone axes from excavated sites and surface collections in Eastern Thrace is still in progress. On the other hand, early results from the Early Neolithic site of Hoca Çeşme, near the town of Enez and the Middle Neolithic site of Yağcılı in the Edirne region showed that the polished stone axes of Hoca Çeşme and Yağcılı were made of rock from the Şarköy sources. Pottery similar to that of Hoca Çeşme also found in Hamaylıtarla. I assume that more axe factory sites exist in the region and probably the axe factories were used from the beginning of the Neolithic to the Bronze Age (see *Box 2*).

Summary and Conclusion

The finding of prehistoric axe factories in Eastern Thrace has aroused much interest in the prehistoric record of the Balkans and Anatolia. All axe factories were found associated with Neolithic and Early Bronze Age settlements. Axe-manufacturing processes consist of an intensive practice of knapping, pecking and polishing. Probably the most important question is how far these axes were distributed from the source? Petrological analysis of the stone axes from Eastern Thrace is still in progress. In the future, we shall be able to define the distributional range of axes from factories. However, early results show that, at the Early Neolithic settlement of Hoca Çeşme and the Late Neolithic site of Yağcılı, stone axes were made of rock from the Şarköy sources.

II-V Problems in the Late Chalcolithic Occupation of Eastern Thrace

In Eastern Thrace prehistory, one of the most important problems is about the Late Chalcolithic occupation. During the millennium from ca. 4500 to 3500 cal. BC, major changes occurred in the East Balkans. These changes occurred in all the aspects of the cultural life (e.g. Chapman 1991). In Northeast Bulgaria, tells such as Ovcharovo, Poljanica, Targoviste and Radingrad are enclosed and defended, with banks and ditches or by palisades, thereby heightening the boundedness of the social groups. Each tells is planned and houses are remarkably large with multiple rooms and entrances (Chapman 1990; Todorova 1986; Bailey 2000). In Durankulak on the Black Sea coast, a new technique of dry-stone wall foundations for post frame houses was identified (Todorova 1989). In this period, very large planned Cucuteni settlements were found in Ukraine and Moldavia. For example, Majdanetskoye is about 270 ha, Talyanki 450 ha and Dobrovody 250 ha (Zbenovich 1996: 207). These enormous settlements contained between 1300 and 2700 houses.

During the Neolithic period of the East Balkans, most dwellings had a domestic function, and in some of them, figurines and cult vessels were found which were used in some form of domestic ritual. This situation changed in the Chalcolithic period, when the differentiation of domestic/private space developed into one of partly public/ritual, partly domestic/private space (Chapman 1991). Chapman (1991) argues that in the East Balkans there is a continuum of ritualization of space, from the house with cult room to the creation of special shrines (e.g. Hotnica: Angelov 1959), to ritual sectors with a complex of household shrines (e.g. the "temple complex" at Dolnoslav: Radunceva 1989). The construction of shines in formerly domestic/private space makes a new way of using and controlling elaborated esoteric knowledge developed by ritual specialists.

There is a trend towards gradually increasing diversity and wealth of grave goods in cemeteries in the East Balkans such as Goljamo Delcevo, Vinica, Devnja, Ovcharovo, Targoviste, Radingrad and Poljanica (Todorova 1986; Chapman 2000a: 168-179; Bailey 2000) (*Fig. V.1*). The trend reaches its peak in the Varna cemetery, where a small number of the 281 graves contain massive concentrations of artefacts in a bewildering array of raw materials (Ivanov 1989). Some 10 cemeteries have been discovered in the Cucuteni-Tripolye culture, the well-known cemetery of Vykhvatintsi. The cemetery consisted of 74 graves with grave goods (Zbenovich 1996: 209). Cemeteries have also been discovered on or near the Black Sea coast in the Hamangia culture (Berciu 1966), most notably in Golovita, Cernovoda and Durankulak (Bailey 2000: 196-197). The East Balkan cemeteries contain rich grave goods made of gold, silver, copper, marble, alabaster, rock crystal, shell, bone and fired clay.

The densification of exchange networks in the Chalcolithic period of the East Balkans took place against the background of the hypothesised increase in productivity. This period is marked by the introduction of a wider range of materials into already existing networks and the certain of an enlarged sphere of prestige goods that tended to be consumed in the contexts of the rituals of the living and dead. There was a dialectical relationship between the prestige of the socio-technique artefacts and the ritual nature of their context of consumption (Chapman 1991; Bailey 2000). This self-reinforcing trend culminated in the ascription of "prime value" to certain metals, such as gold and silver (Renfrew 1986). The production of prestige goods as well as artefacts of prime value was an additional route towards increasing status differentiation. It is the expansion of socio-political alliances rooted in lineage power with its ideological power dispersed through a number of ritual centres and based on economic power gained through intensified surplus production channelled into far-flung exchange networks (Chapman 1991).

Fig. V.1. Map of the Balkans, showing selected the Late Chalcolithic sites

One documented aspect of exchange network in the East Balkans is copper exchance. During the Chalcolithic period in the Balkans there is a major role in large-scale extraction and distribution of copper. Copper was mined extensively, especially at Ai Bunar in South-Central Bulgaria and Rudna Glava in Serbia (Jovanović 1976; Černych 1978). However, recent lead isotope analyses from tells close to the Ai Bunar mine show that the vast majority of tools from these tells were made of copper introduced from Northwest of Bulgaria (Pernicka *et al.* 1993). In addition, the lead isotope analyses of copper object from the Durankulak cemetery show that objects made of copper derived from different sources (Chapman 2000a: 124). The Late

50

Chalcolithic period has also witnessed the use of the marine mollusc Spondylus and Dentalium as raw materials. A significant numbers of Spondylus were found in the Varna and Durankulak cemeteries (Todorova 1986). Spondylus was probably an Aegean mollusc and it was also found at Macedonian sites, such as Sitagroi and Dikili Tash (Bailey 2000). A total of 212 finished rings, beads and buttons made of Spondylus and 63 pieces of waste or unfinished samples were found at Dimini in Greece (Halstead 1993; Séfériadés 2000). During the Late Chalcolithic period, exchange networks must have played an important part in the acquisition of raw materials.

The Late Chalcolithic period (ca. 4500-3800 cal. BC) of Eastern Thrace is marked by a decrease in the number of the settlements. All known settlements are small and low relative to those of other Late Chalcolithic Cultures in the Balkans. Surface finds from Eastern Thrace, belonging to this period is unsophisticated. The apparent dramatic decrease in population of Eastern Thrace in the Late Chalcolithic period is one of the major research problems in the region, and suggests that we are facing a pattern of regional significance.

Changes during the Late Chalcolithic period in Eastern Thrace and Explanatory Models

Until now, the Late Chalcolithic period in Eastern Thrace was largely *terra incognita*. Our surveys in the Edirne region have provided important evidence relating the Late Chalcolithic Occupation. Until our investigations, the limited excavations at the sites of Tilkiburnu and Kanligeçit in the Kırklareli region were the only serious attempt to address issues of the Late Chalcolithic occupation in Eastern Thrace. The disturbed site of Tilkiburnu was investigated in 1981 by Özdoğan (Özdoğan 1982). The site had been damaged by the dig of a large trench and also by a concrete gun-post. Vessels were collected in 4 pits in the section along the destruction trench (Özdoğan 1982). Özdoğan argues that the pottery from Tilkiburnu bears some similarities to the Karanovo VI- Gumelniţa Culture of the Balkans (Özdoğan 1982). However, some characteristic features of Gumelniţa are absent from Tilkiburnu. Özdoğan dated Tilkiburnu to a transitional period between the Chalcolithic and the Early Bronze Age (Özdoğan 1999a: 10). The Kanligeçit excavations, near the town of Kırklareli have revealed typical Kocatepe pottery together with some sherds resembling Karanovo VI-Gumelniţa pottery. Fine black burnished ware, red mottled ware with stroke-burnish decoration, medium fine light grey coloured unburnished ware and red slipped burnished ware are characteristic ware types. Incurved rim bowls are a common shape. All Kanlıgaçit pottery comes from pits. Kocatepe pottery and some Karanovo VI have been found together in these pits, and Karanovo VI pottery of Kanlıgeçit has not been found in any site in Eastern Thrace. It is possible that these pits can be dated to the very end of the Maritsa culture. Thus, Kanligeçit may be dated to the end of the Maritsa culture and the beginning of the Karanovo VI- Gumelniţa culture. Özdoğan believes that there are no Late Chalcolithic settlements existents in Turkish Thrace, only cultural remains deposited in pits (Özdoğan 1998a). However, our investigations in the Edirne region proved that this idea is incorrect. During our survey in the Edirne region, four Late Chalcolithic settlements were found - Kavakli 1, Yumurta Tepe, Karabaş and Tepeyanı (see *Fig. B.1*). A careful typological analysis of the pottery from these settlements shows chronologically two different phases (Erdoğu 2002). It seems the Karabaş pottery is earlier than others and it shows remarkable similarities to the Drama Karanovo VI pottery (e.g. Lichardus *et al.* 2000: Abb.25;6,8,11 ; Fol *et al.* 1989: Taf.6;1). Some Karabaş types of fine sherds were also found at Tepeyanı. On the other hand, Nearly all the parallels for Yumurta Tepe and Kavakli I as well as some Tepeyanı pottery point to the second, third and fourth phases of the Krivodol-Salcuţa-Bubanj Culture and the last phase of the Gumelniţa-Karanovo VI Culture of the Balkans (Georgieva 1990; Todorova 1978). The similarities are especially apparent in the types of decoration, but also to some extent in the repertoire of shapes (Erdoğu 1999b; 2002). On the basis of pottery evidence, I suggested that (Erdoğu 2002) the pottery from Eastern Thrace was the product of local development, which is closely related to the Karanovo VI-Gumelniţa and Krivodol-Salcuţa cultures (*Fig. V.2-3*).

Fig. V.2. Pottery from Karabaş (top) and Yumurta Tepe (bottom)

Fig. V.3. Pottery from Kavaklı (top) and Tepeyanı (bottom)

Karanovo VI settlements in the Edirne region have the smallest size range compared with the Neolithic and the Early Bronze Age. The relationship between site size and maximum sherd density is seen in *Fig. V.4*. The largest site is Kavaklı 1, about 45.000 square meters in size, and Tepeyanı is the smallest Karanovo VI site, about 4.800 square meters in size.

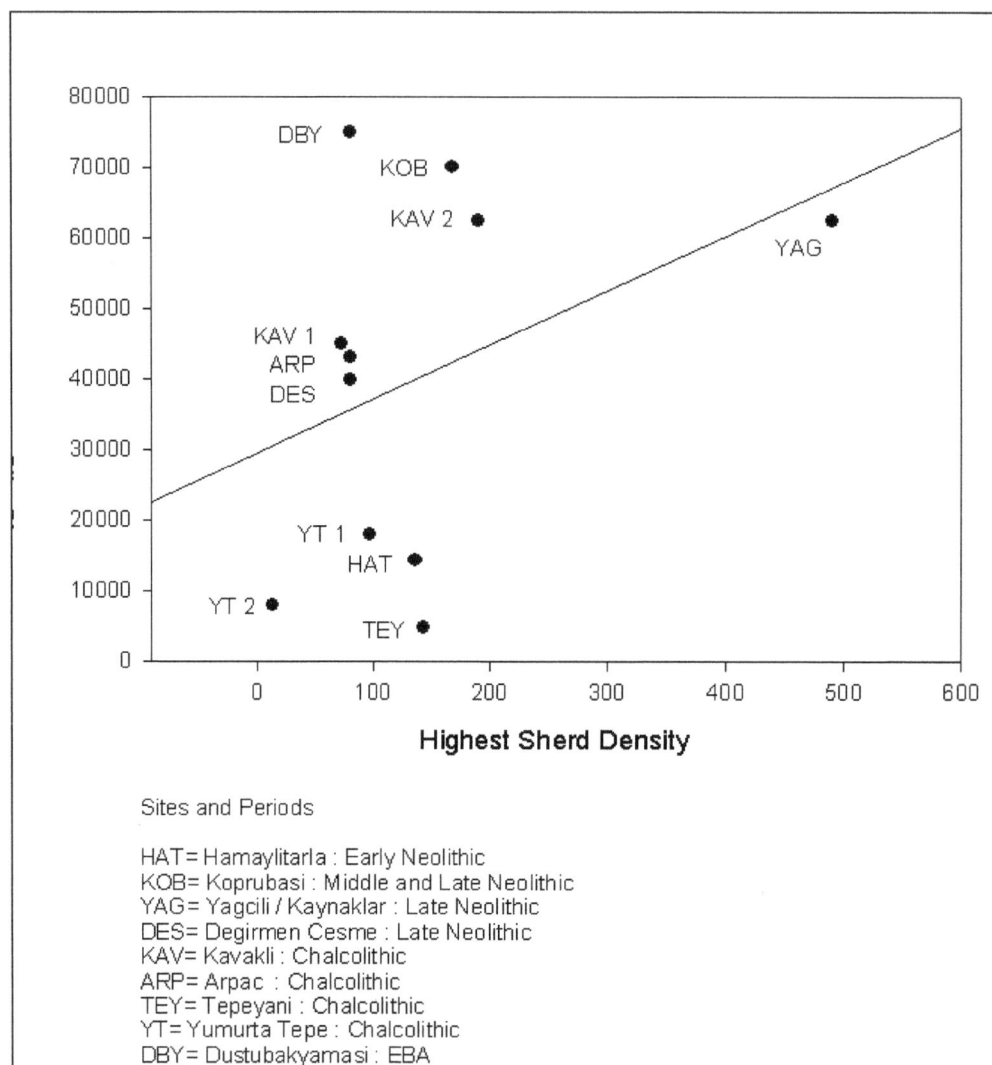

Sites and Periods

HAT = Hamaylitarla : Early Neolithic
KOB = Koprubasi : Middle and Late Neolithic
YAG = Yagcili / Kaynaklar : Late Neolithic
DES = Degirmen Cesme : Late Neolithic
KAV = Kavakli : Chalcolithic
ARP = Arpac : Chalcolithic
TEY = Tepeyani : Chalcolithic
YT = Yumurta Tepe : Chalcolithic
DBY = Dustubakyamasi : EBA

Fig. V.4. Site size vs. highest sherd density in settlements of the Edirne region

The apparent decrease in population and occurrence of small settlements with unsophisticated artefacts in Eastern Thrace in the Late Chalcolithic period may be explained by several processes. On the other hand, intensive archaeological surveys were conducted over only a small part of Eastern Thrace, so it is possible that one big Late Chalcolithic site has been missed. One explanation concerns climatic changes. However, it is not clear whether climatic changes were the direct cause of depopulation of Eastern Thrace in the Late Chalcolithic period.

Lamb argues that climatic changes occurred in 4500-3500/3000 cal. BC (Lamb 1982: 29). This period is characterised by increases in temperature. During the summer, the temperature was 1 to 3 C° higher than today (Lamb 1982). According to Todorova, climatic changes occurred at the end of the Chalcolithic period, not at the beginning (Todorova 1993; 1995). She argues that at the end of the fifth millennium BC, the final stage of climate optimum, when mean annual temperatures reached their maximum of 3 C° higher, this was a catastrophic event for Southeast Europe (Todorova 1995: 89). The rising sea level caused the water table to rise, resulting in the flooding of the plains. According to Huntley who works on   the relationships between vegetational changes and climatic changes in Europe, 'the Quercus-Pinus sclerophyll forests of Southeast Europe have increasing abundance of several major sclerophyll taxa since 8000 BP with some taxa peaking in abundance ca. 2000 BP'(Huntley 1990: 516). These changes imply increasing temperatures in Southeast Europe since 8000 BP. The reduction in annual rainfall may also relate to increase in temperature. Changes in annual distribution of rainfall could have caused a decline in agricultural production. One important point is that increases in temperature can be expected to lengthen the growing season in some regions where agricultural potential is currently limited (Tagart et al. 1990). This means, increases in temperature affects different regions in different ways. Increases in temperature also affect the crop calendar. Temperature increases may extent the geographic range of some insect pests currently limited by temperature (Tegart et al. 1990). Most agricultural diseases have greater potential to reach severe levels under warmer conditions. Perhaps most important for agriculture are the possible changes in climatic variability, such as the magnitude and frequency of droughts, storms, heat waves and severe frosts (Tegart et el. 1990). The apparent increases in mean annual temperatures in regions could sufficiently increase heat stress on crops. Climatic changes may affect crop and livestock productivity in Turkish Thrace, because the main temperatures in the Edirne region are higher than in East Bulgaria, and the annual rainfall is lower than in East Bulgaria (see Yordanov 1938-39). This means increases in temperature may affect the Edirne region more than other regions in the East Balkans. However, there are, as yet, no detailed geomorphological studies and no pollen diagrams for Eastern Thrace.

Climatic changes can also be directly related to changes in the coastal morphology of the Black Sea and the Sea of Marmara. The Black sea is linked to the Aegean by the Sea of Marmara and two small straits; Dardanelles and Bosphorus. During the regression periods of the Mediterranean in the Pleistocene, the straits were blocked by land, thus the Black Sea and the Sea of Marmara were no more than fresh water lakes with considerably lower levels than today (Erinç 1954; Deuser 1972; Degens and Ross 1974; Gunterson and Özturgut 1974; Stanley and Blanpied 1980; Özdoğan 1985b; Özdoğan in press; Ryan and Pitman 1998; Ballard et al. 2001). The first intrusion of warm and saline waters from the Aegean to the Sea of Marmara took place in the 6th millennium BC., soon to be followed by the establishment of a link with the Black Sea, that lasted until the sea level was 3 to 5 m higher than today. On the base of the core samples from the Sea of Marmara, Stanley and Blanpied (1980: 539) argued that 'between 9500 and 7500 BP... The continued eastward overflow of saline Mediterranean water across the Dardanelles spread along density interfaces in the Eastern Marmara basin, and water above the bottom remained partially, and at times completely, euxinic. The continued rapid eustatic sea-level rise during this period also enables minor amounts of Mediterranean waters to cross the Bosphorus and overflow into the Black Sea'. The alternating growth and shrinkage of ice sheets probably resulted changes in the coastal morphology of the Black Sea and the Sea of Marmara (van Andel 1989). There is also empirical evidence of climate change and tectonic activity (Macklin et al. 1995).

The recent work of Ryan and Pitman in the Black Sea indicates that, about 7500 years ago, sea-level of the Black Sea raised suddenly. Radiocarbon dating of the shells of the first salt-tolerant molluscan invaders from the Mediterranean yielded the age of ca. 7550 BP. (Ryan and Pitman et al. 1997; Ryan and Pitman 1998). But some researchers argue that Ryan and Pitman date the flood to the same radiocarbon age as the first sediments laid down after the flooding, which were black and organic-rich and therefore formed in conditions lacking oxygen. Thus the flooding may in fact have occurred earlier (Kerr 1998: 1132). The recent investigations in the Gulf of Izmit show that the initial connection between the Black Sea and the Sea of Marmara could have been through the Izmit-Sapanca Basin, and not through the present Bosphorus (Meriç 1995; Özdoğan in press). This channel was blocked by the rapid advance of the Sakarya delta during the beginning of the 4th millennium BC (Stanley and Blanpied 1980: 541; Özdoğan in press). What happened later is not clear, but the archaeological evidences from Bulgaria and Western Georgia indicate that the Black Sea had a considerable regression between 4850 and

4000 BP. (Draganov 1995; Shilik 1997: 117). Along the Bulgarian coast of the Black Sea about 12 submerged sites dating from the Chalcolithic to the Early Bronze II period have been found at the depth of 4 to 8 m below present sea-level (Draganov 1995; Özdoğan in press). At Calchis in Western Georgia, a sample of peat from a depth of 8-8,5 m has been radiocarbon dated to 4130 BP (Shilik 1997: 117). All these evidences indicate that during the end of the 3rd millennium BC the coastal morphology of the Black Sea changed, because of sudden rising of sea level. On the other hand, Sozopol excavations showed that at the end of the fifth millennium BC, the Black sea also raised (Draganov 1995: 235). The archaeological evidence from the Western Georgia show that after the end of the 3rd millennium BC, changes of the sea-level of the Black Sea still continues (Shilik 1997). Evidince from the bottom sediments of both the Black Sea and the Sea of Marmara indicated that the present conditions were established only by the 1st millennium BC. (Stanley and Blanpied 1980: 541; Özdoğan 1997: 29).

Soil condition is another explanation of depopulation of Eastern Thrace during the Late Chalcolithic period. In response to increasing drought conditions the soils in Eastern Thrace may have become poorer. However, no soil analysis has been done in Eastern Thrace and consequently no evidence support this hypothesis. On the other hand, examinations in the Nova Zagora region of Bulgaria show how soil conditions changed during the prehistoric period. In the Nova Zagora region, an abrupt soil change happened during the Early Bronze Age (Dennell and Webley 1975). For instance, at Ezero there is a sharp difference between the Late Neolithic and Early Bronze Age soils. A light - coloured, similar to the eroded form of the Cinnomonic Forest soil has changed to a dark and heavier riverine clay, which is not so suitable for crop cultivation (Dennell and Webley 1975: 101). According to Dennell and Webley, many tell settlements were abandoned because of the deposition of such clay formations (1975: 101).

The occurrence of small settlements with unsophisticated artefacts in Eastern Thrace in the Late Chalcolithic period may be explained by an "attraction model". When there are negative social or economic conditions in one region and positive conditions in another region, people often perceived that the best opportunities for their development lay in migration to a region with positive conditions. The reason for such movements may be explained by regional conflicts, disease, famine, religious need or economic collapse. Anthony (1997: 25) pointed out that migrants often seem simply to move to places that are familiar and offer social support, rather than moving to the place that would mark the best economic choice. People do not move about randomly, but follow kin and co-residents to places that have an attractive reputation.

The decrease in the number of settlements and the occurrence of a few small Late Chalcolithic settlements in Eastern Thrace may also be explained by the collapse of the exchange network. The East Balkans had a great development of the economic, social, political and symbolic life in the Chalcolithic period. The production of prestige goods as well as artefacts of prime value made of gold, copper and the marine shells was an important route towards increasing status differentiation. Lineage and ideological power based on economic power gained through intensified surplus production channelled into long-distance exchange networks. In the Late Chalcolithic period, exchange networks shifted the economic, political and ideological core to the East Balkans. It is possible that East Balkan "power" created links between exchange and value, and powerful groups controlled the distribution of prestige goods as well as artefacts of prime value. EasternThrace has copper sources in the Istranca Mountain. A small gold source was also found at Slivarovo (Archibald 1998:23), Vaysal and Iğneada in the Istranca Mountains. A large number of malachite beads were found in the Middle and Late Neolithic levels of Aşağı Pınar (Özdoğan and Parzinger 2000). There are, as yet, no excavated Chalcolithic sites in Eastern Thrace. Copper was mined extensively in the south Bulgaria and especially Serbia, and Chalcolithic people were supplied with copper from these regions (Pernicka et al. 1993). On the other hand, Wagner and Özturnali (2000:33) suggested that copper was mined in prehistoric times at two locations – Derekoy and Ikiztepe- in the Kirklareli region of Turkish Thrace. The primary sources of silver are also in north-Western Bulgaria. When long-distance exchange networks developed in the east Balkans, - cf. north-eastern Bulgaria or Moldavia - some regions, such as the upper Ergene basin of Eastern Thrace, lost their importance.

It is assumed that there is a spatial dimension to kinship relations in most Neolithic and Chalcolithic social networks. Hence, local exchange networks are dominated by exchange between kinfolk. Chapman (2000a: 34) argues that the pattern of artefact distributions in the Balkan Neolithic and Chalcolithic gives little support for the notion of closed marriage networks. There is a high probability that overlapping marriage networks channelled access to wider, non-kinship-based exchange networks. In Balkan prehistory, the distribution of goods from sources to people desiring them may imply one of two possibilities; a wider set of non-kin-based barter networks or an extended suite of kin-based enchained relations (Chapman 2000a:34). Long-distance exchange becomes so important for maintaining the social structure of local communities. Objects of great value were received primarily through networks of transactions conducted with non-kin rather than with kinsfolk or neighbours. If some goods with a high social value were distributed between neighbours or kin, this took place in completely different social contexts. It is possible that the complexities of enchained relations across long distances may well result in a collapse of the exchange network or, at least a partial reduction in size.

There are no detailed investigations about Late Neolithic exchange networks of Eastern Thrace. Thus it is impossible to determinate how already existing networks collapse. A large number of malachite beads and Aegean Spondylus, were found in the Late Neolithic levels of Aşağı Pınar (Özdoğan 1999a; Özdoğan and Parzinger 2000). At the Late Neolithic settlement of Yağcılı in the Edirne region, a stone axe from the Şarköy factories was found. These examples may show an exchange network in the Late Neolithic period of Turkish Thrace.

Summary and Conclusion

The apparent dramatic decrease in population of Eastern Thrace during the Late Chalcolithic period still poses a problem. Only a number of Late Chalcolithic settlements were found in Eastern Thrace, and they have the smallest size range compared with Neolithic ang Early Bronze Age settlements. The occurrence of small settlements with unsophisticated artefacts in this period may be explained by climatic changes, soil changes or exchange network collapse. It is not yet clear whether network collapse was due to political events or gemorphological changes or some other factors.

II-VI VISUALIZING NEOLITHIC LANDSCAPE SYMBOLISM FOR ISLAND COLONIZATION

In south-east European prehistory, the transition from foraging to farming is one of the most important periods of cultural change yet; it remains the subject of conflicting opinions. Certainly, it cannot be doubted that the Aegean islands are one of the key regions for understanding this cultural change. Specific models about Aegean island colonization have been developed by several authors (e.g. Cherry 1984; 1990; Patton 1996; Broodbank 1999; 2000). Cherry (1990) suggested that the first colonization of the Aegean islands was by farming groups, and post-dated by millennia earlier indications of foraging maritime exploration. He also suggested a distinction between colonization and discovering or visiting (1984). A community may know of the existence of an island and may visit it periodically without actually colonising it. On the basis of ethnographic evidence, Cherry also suggested movement of flocks to summer grazing on islands (Cherry 1985: 20). This could have led gradually to the settlement of some of Aegean islands.

McArthur and Wilson (1967) proposed the island biogeography model which argued colonization of island by the mainland package of domesticates - plants and animals. The key variables identified by McArthur and Wilson are island size and distance from the mainland. Larger islands contain greater amounts of species and resources, and small, distant islands should have the least biodiversity and natural resources. Island size could be divided by distance from the mainland to give an area/distance (A/DR) ratio. The A/DR ratio favours variables that pertain to the likelihood that an island will be colonized. Held suggested that target width is a more meaningful variable than size (quoted in Patton 1996: 40). Target width is defined as the angle which an island subtends on the horizon when viewed from the staging area for a colonization, may be divided by distance from staging point to give a target/distance (T/D) ratio. The T/D ratio favours geographic variables related to insular discovery.

Alternatively, Broodbank argued that 'in the Neolithic and EBA Aegean, where a long prior tradition of island visitation can be inferred, and where levels of island inter-visibility are high in good weather conditions, T/D ratios are in general less useful than in areas where long-range over-the-horizon voyaging is basic to colonisation sequences' (Broodbank 2000: 136-137). Patton has emphasized the expected patterns that islands with higher biographic ranking should be colonized first, while islands with a higher T/D ratio are more likely to be discovered first (Patton 1996: 45).

Taking into account the result of geomorpological analysis, the vast majority of Aegean land-loss occurred with the first c. 80-90 m of sea-level rise, which correlates with the latest Upper Palaeolithic and the Mesolithic (Lambeck 1996). According to Broodbank (1999: 22), bathymetric and eustatic information suggest that several substantial Aegean islands, as well as innumerable off-shore islets, only become separated from the mainland at a relatively late stage of sea-level rise. Several Aegean islands could have been undergoing gradual insularization at the time immediately before or in the Neolithic period. On the basis of the size and distance index, Broodbank introduced a model of early colonization of super-attractive islands (1999). According to him, super-attractive islands were colonized first.

In their discussion of the colonization of islands, Keegan and Diamond (1987: 52) suggested that close islands were colonised before distant islands and big islands were colonized before small islands. Islands were colonized by people closest to them. The large islands close to the mainland with many natural resources were probably attractive for Early Neolithic communities. According to Keegan and Diamond's concept of autocatalysis, coastal and island configuration may encourage initial island settlement as well as later expansion (1987: 67-68).

Broodbank's model (1999) also applies the concepts of seafaring nurseries and of autocatalysis to the Aegean's coasts and islands in order to locate specific zones that would encourage island settlement and expansion.

Archaeologists working in the Aegean Islands generally accepted that there has been no evidence for early farming communities in the Eastern Aegean islands (Cherry 1990; Davis 1992: 702; Perlés 2001: 61). However, an Early Neolithic settlement was recently found on the island of Gökçeada –Imbroz - (Harmankaya and Erdoğu 2001). None of the colonization models indicates that Gökçeada is the most promising island for early colonization (see also Broodbank 1999: 30), so why did Early Neolithic people settle on this island? I would like to suggest a different idea, related to the symbolic value of landscape for island colonization. I agree with Robb (2001) that islands are more than physical land surrounded by water. Islands are ideas-inhabited metaphors, natural symbols of boundedness and separation. Islands are locales forming the focus in the symbolic construction of meaning.

Sense of Place and Place-myths

Place commonly refers to a defined area, a fixed location (Relph 1976: 8). However, places are always far more than a definite area or locations, because they have distinctive meanings and values for persons (Tilley 1994: 15; Chapman 1998: 108). The relationships between space and place have been discussed by a number of 'humanistic geographers', such as Yi-Fu Tuan (1977), who suggests that the notion of place is arbitrary, elusive and protean. Tuan sees the identity of place as having two distinct forms. Places are locations in which people have long memories lasting generations. Places are also centres of power, as well as meaning, relative to their environs, the node at which activities converge. Tuan also pointed out that the power of symbols in places is dependent upon the depth of the human emotions experienced in the field of care and public symbols which provide significance in wider, public milieu.

Most significant places are located or positioned in space. Locales are places created and known through common experiences, symbols and meaning (Tilley 1994: 18). Locales may offer a distinct quality of being inside, or part of, a place. People both live out their lives in place and have a sense of being part of it. People and places are hard to separate because the identity of a person is tied to that of his or her place. A sense of attachment to place is frequently derived from the stability of meanings associated with it (Tilley 1994: 18). A sense of place is formed through the sedimentation of symbolic and emotional meanings, memories and the attachments to people and things, which arise out of past practices and their underlying power relations. According to Strathern (1988: 175), the objectification of place-value and place meaning by users is not only related to the places themselves but also the identity of the places and of the persons who use and inhabit the places.

Each person effectively reshapes a place by making his or her story a thread in the meaning of the place. Shields (1991: 46-47) argues that communal mythology is formed by a set of place-myths. Place-myths represent the conflicting but often internally coherent visions of the identity of a particular place. Place-myths consist of a collective set of place-images. Place-images derive from face-to-face encounters with particular places and consist of discrete meanings associated with real places regardless of their character in reality. People conjure up images of place and these images generally contain mountains, rocky outcrops, lakes, caves or forests.

Ethnographic evidence from Australia shows that Aboriginal people in Arnhem Land move seasonally to the Crocodile islands to use marine resources. They have sacred sites in the islands, and these sites may take the form of depressions in the land surface, areas devoid of vegetation, rocky outcrops, reefs, underwater caves, sand ridges, freshwater springs, particular shapes in land features and distinct vegetational patterns (S. Davis 1989: 50). These sites are also held to be dangerous, except to those protected by ritual knowledge and status. These places have their own stories and are associated with the ancestral beings.

Places may be perpetuated through devices such as myths and legends, which in turn serve to stimulate memories and mental images at odds with what is observed. Myths enable a community to establish a sense of belonging within a landscape. I would suggest that such myths linking particular places may guide early farming societies on journeys around the places which they exploited. Particular places are also very important 'landmarks' in the landscape that links the movement of individuals or communities. Broodbank has already suggested that islanders or - I might add people living by the sea - employed mental maps to locate distance points, in which travelling time, directions and landmarks were remembered in sequence (Broodbank 2000: 23). In navigation, as well as experience and knowledge, stories (both real and mythic) also play important role. The nineteenth-century Cambridge Expedition to Torres Strait in the Pacific showed that 'the natives have a strongly marked appreciation of geographical features and can readily make maps or potray the essential characteristics of an island from memory' (Haddon 1912: 229).

Visuality and Cognitive Mapping

As Tuan (1977) argues, the eyes explore the visual field and abstraction from it certain objects, point of focus, perspectives. Thus study of landscape visualization concerns not only the reality of landscape, but also the images derived as repositories of place meaning formed and interpreted in the mind. Complexity in landscape is a function of violated expectations. Environmental complexity exists when noticeable differences are recognized in the face of more simplistic anticipations. When these differences overwhelm the accepted, the mind becomes confused and must seek different memory patterns to interpret the scene.

Higuchi gave eight criteria for determining the visual structure of a place (1989: 4).
1.	Visibility or invisibility: This concerns the fundamental question of what can be seen and what cannot be seen from a given viewpoint.
2.	Distance: This has to do with the changes that take place in the appearance of an object as the distance between the observer and the object varies.
3.	Angle and incidence. When a landscape is conceived of as a concatenation of surfaces, the angle at which the line of vision strikes each surface determines to a large degree what can be seen of it. This index evaluates the comparative visibility of the various surfaces in a given landscape.
4.	Depth and invisibility: This gauges the degree of invisibility in terms of the depth of the unseen section with respect to the line of vision.
5.	Angle of depression: This clarifies the viewer's sense of position as s/he looks at a scene from above.
6.	Angle of elevation: This indicates the nature of the upward view and the limits of visible space.
7.	Depth: This clarifies the degree of three-dimensionality of the landscape as it unfolds before the viewer.
8.	Light: The appearance of a landscape changes drastically in accordance with the manner in which the light strikes it. This index has to do with the transformations that take place as the position of the source of light moves from front to side to back.'

Memory is complex in that it is a combination of mental acts such as recognition, recall and articulation (Fentress and Wickham 1992: 26). To recognize something is to be able to identify it using previous knowledge, while recall is internal remembrance involving some form of mental pictures. Mental pictures garnered from the landscape are synthesized as a person's personal geography. These pictures may be generated through memories of actual experiences or through secondary perception and the transformation of received images. Schama (1995: 15) argues that mental pictures do not exist and can never actually be found in reality quite as they are visualized in the mind, yet they constitute the images that serve to represent what has been or can be experienced. Cognitive mapping keeps people oriented to their surroundings so that movement becomes purposive. A cognitive map of prehistoric people consists of visual aspects of environmental experiences. Gibson (1979: 75-76) correctly argues that visualization plays an important role in movement.

The landscape surrounding villages provides locales, or places the focus in the metaphorical constriction of meaning. Tilley (1999: 178) argues that 'places, and the stories associated with them, almost inevitably become metaphors involved in a discourse about relationships between individuals and groups. Through talking about place one can remind others of social obligations with regard to kith and kin. As such places in the landscape forge individual and collective biographies and shared histories through presses of metaphoric construction creating meaning in the world. Cultures differentially name the kinds of places (streams, mountains) and specific places that are significant to them'. The collective memory is the abstracted essence of an event or story that a group holds because of their common experience of witnessing or visualising the event (Halbwachs 1980). It is by communicating, by remembering a shared memory within a group that a memory is corroborated and maintained. People recognize, inscribe and collectively maintain certain places or regions in ritual, symbolic or ceremonial, which these places create and express sociocultural identity (Knapp and Ashmore 1999); places like islands that provide panoramic views or large vistas of interesting and varied landscape features.

I suggest that Early Neolithic communities on the coast of Western Anatolia obviously knew of the existence of islands and may have visited them periodically or may have moved to them seasonally for animal breeding, grazing or fishing expeditions, with occupying fixed settlements. These fixed settlements may have had cosmological significance, as a key location in an ancestor-myth or cosmological scheme, and are derived from visual experience. Later, after these ancestor-myths were told and re-told, perhaps over generations, the symbolic value of the islands may have become more important. This could have led to the permanent settlement of some islands. Ancestors probably also played an important role for sedentism.

The Early Neolithic sites in Western Anatolia and Eastern Aegean Islands

The earliest known pottery culture in Western Anatolia is characterized by red-slipped burnished ware. This type of ware has also been found in a number of settlements throughout Western Thrace as well as in Turkish Thrace (Harmankaya *et al.* 1997). The Early Neolithic of Western Anatolia is characterized by two different zones; the interior and the littoral (*Fig. VI.1*). The interior settlements are generally situated on the edge of fertile alluvial plains that are good for agriculture and the side valleys of main rivers such as Gediz and Büyük Menderes (e.g. Moralı, Nuriye and Killiktepe), although some sites are located in small valleys that command small areas of cultivable land (e.g. Tepeüstü). Settlements in the littoral region are different. In general settlements are situated immediately on the Aegean coast. For example Tavşan Adası is situated on an islet, c. 80 m from the coast (Akdeniz 1997: 262). Saplı Adası is also situated on a small peninsula or islet (Akdeniz 1997: 263). Coşkuntepe lies on a small natural hill close to the sea, with no cultivable land (Seeher 1990). Ege Gübre also has a similar location. There are as yet no excavations or detailed geomorphological investigations. However, the littoral settlements suggest that agriculture may not have been the dominant subsistence strategy (Thissen 2000), which may be related to fishing and stock breeding. Probably the people living in these settlements had maritime navigational skills. Perlès (1992; 2001: 207) suggests that Melos obsidian was distributed by groups of specialized seafarers, and that a single trip to Melos, bringing back several kilograms of obsidian, could easy fulfil the yearly needs of many villages (2001: 208). The littoral settlements may have exchanged obsidian and other raw materials from the sea with agricultural products from inland settlements. For example, Melian obsidian was found at the inland settlement of Morali (Renfrew *et al.* 1965: Tab.1. no: 137 &

138). I already suggested (2003b: 12) that early Hoca Çeşme dates c. 6500-6200 cal. BC (Thissen 2002; Erdogu *et al.* 2003), may also be applied for the whole Western Anatolian Early Neolithic culture.

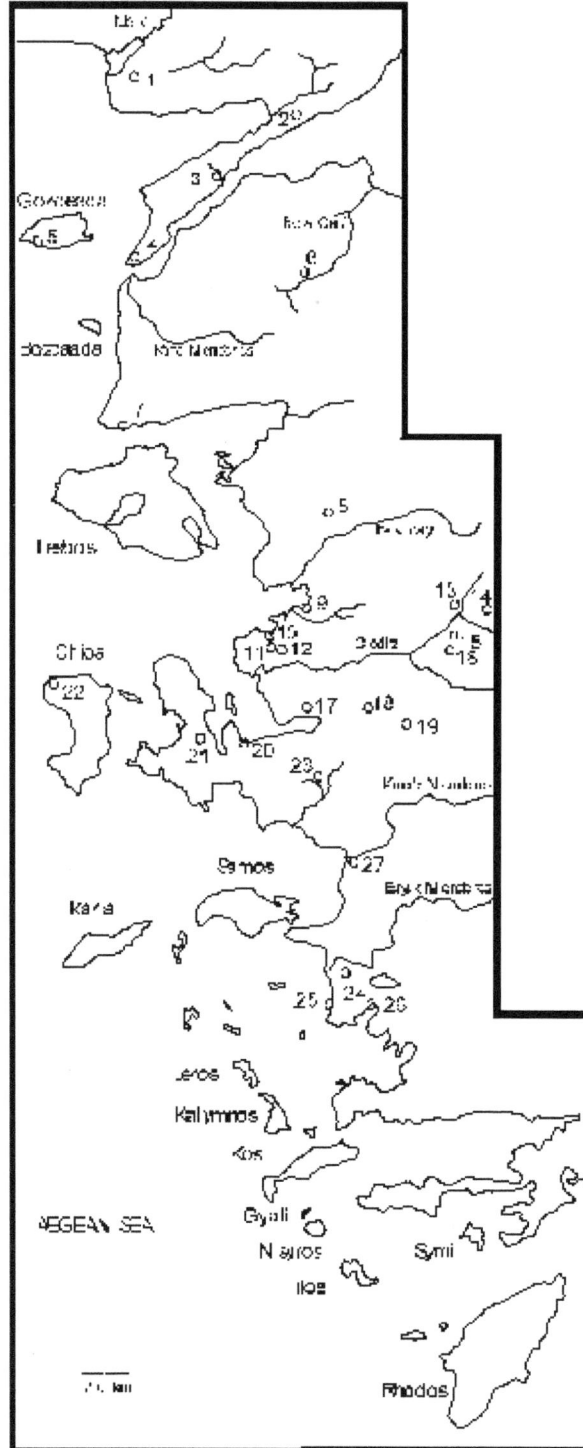

Fig. VI.1. Location map of Early Neolithic sites in Western Anatolia 1.Hoca Cesme, 2.Hamaylitarla, 3.Kaynarca, 4.Karaagactepe, 5.Ugurlu, 6.Calca, 7.Coskuntepe,8.Pasaköy 9.Caltidere ,10.Ege Gubre, 11.Araptepe,12 Höyücek II,13.Kayislar,14.Morali,15.Nuriye,16.Alibey,17.Küçük Yamanlar,18.Ulucak,19.Nemrut,20.Limantepe,21.Tepeüstü-Barbaros,22.Ayio Gala,23.Tepeköy, 24.Killiktepe,25.Tavsanadasi,26.Sapliada 27.Efes Cukuriçi.

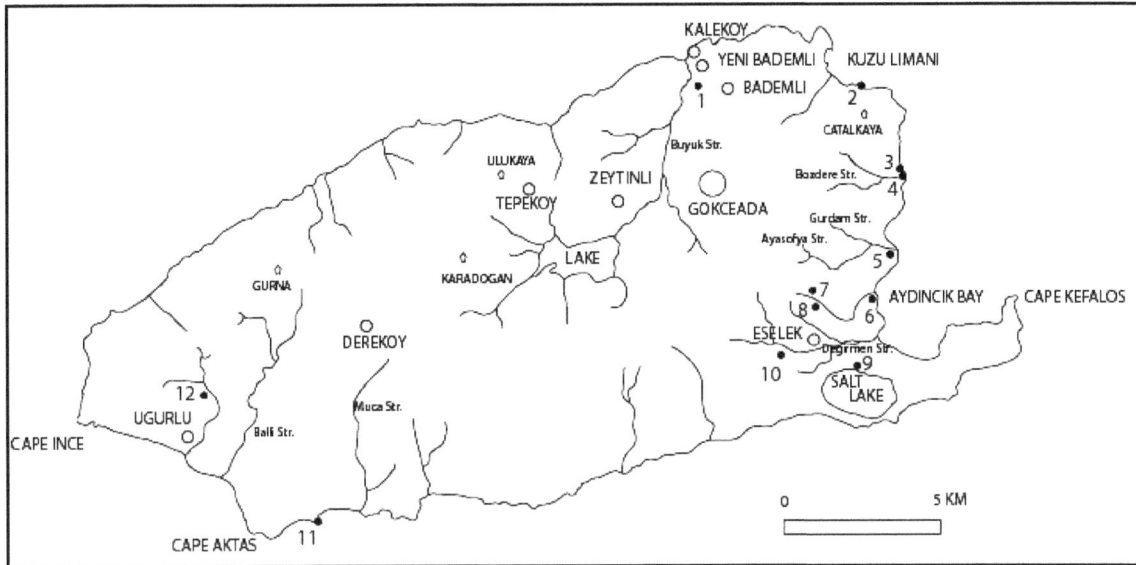

Fig. VI.2. Location map of Prehistoric sites in the Island of Gökçeada
1.Bedemli, 2.Uçburun, 3.Kalamya, 4.Vaniyeri, 5.Kukuvaki,
6.Incirlik Kiyisi, 7.Eselek Cave, 8.Eskino Yamaci, 9.Sirma, 10.Peri Cave, 11.Pirgos, 12.Ugurlu.

The island of Gökçeada is about 17 km from the Gelibolu Peninsula. During our survey, the Western Anatolian type material was found at Uğurlu (Harmankaya and Erdoğu 2003; Erdoğu 2003b). Uğurlu is a low mound c. 1 km northeast of the village of Uğurlu in the western part of the island of Gökçeada (*Fig.VI.2*). It is c. 2.5 km from the sea, and commands fairly extensive cultivable lands to the South (*Fig. VI.3*). It was first discovered in 1997 and re-visited in 1999 by S. Harmankaya, during his extensive survey of the island (Harmankaya and Erdoğu 2001). Surface finds of Early Neolithic data cover an area of c. 100x100 m. The Early Neolithic pottery from Uğurlu is identical to that found in Western Anatolian settlements. All the pottery is tempered with small grit, mica, chaff and sand and is typically thin-walled. Red and black coloured slips are applied on surfaces. Red slip sherds are dominant and sometimes are brown and orange mottled. All sherds are well burnished. S-shaped bowls, vertically placed tubular lugs, bead rims, flat and ring bases are commonly occurring. Vertically placed very long tubular lugs are also attested. There is also a piece of a zoomorphic vessel. Apart from the pottery, chipped stone implements were also collected. The main raw materials used in the chipped stone industry consist mainly of flint. No obsidian was found. Retouched blades are among the significant tool types.

The Western Anatolian type material was found at Ayio Gala Cave on the island of Chios. The pottery from the lower cave and the early layers of upper cave is similar to Western Anatolian Early Neolithic pottery; red and grey slipped, well burnished and thin-walled, tempered with grit, chaff or mica. It is often mottled, shading to brown and orange. These characteristics are also dominant in Hoca Çeşme (Özdoğan 1998b), Moralı and Coşkuntepe (personal observation). The shapes of the vessels also show close similarities to Western Anatolian settlement wares (see Erdoğu 2003b). Figurines found at Ayio Gala already have been compared to Anatolia (e.g. Hacilar) and the Early Neolithic settlements in Greece (Hood 1981: 63-66; Zachos 1996). Bone smoothers from Ayio Gala (Hood 1981: Fig.45; 341; Plate 12a) have close parallels with those from Early Neolithic settlements such as Hoca Çeşme (Özdoğan 1999b: Fig.23).

Visual structure of Aegean islands

The littoral Neolithic settlements in Western Anatolia are situated immediately on the Aegean coast. Among them Coşkuntepe is situated on the northern part of Western Anatolia, at the closest point (9 km) to the island of Lesbos. It is situated on a small natural hill, rising vertically from the sea, about 1 km from a small bay, with no cultivable land. Lesbos is a mountainous island, and the mountain (Lepetimnos: 980 m) opposite Coşkuntepe is a spectacular feature (*Fig. VI.4*). I believe that the choice of this location is not a coincidence. Some of Higuchi's criteria may also apply to Coşkuntepe. Visibility: Coşkuntepe is situated at the closest point to the island that the whole north-eastern part of the island is visible. This part of the island has a harmonious, well-arranged combination of aesthetic and geometric forms. Distance: in the near-distance, the mountain constitutes the principal element in the landscape. Angle of incidence: the mountain has slopes of more than 30 degrees. The slopes are very steep and present a wide angle of incidence to the viewer. Depth: the landscape consists of three-dimensional spaces in which some objects are nearer and some farther away from the viewer. When the air is dry and clears the island and its mountain appears to be close by. When the air is misty the island appears to be far away. Light: the appearance of the mountain changes during the sunset, and during foggy days one can see the island as if hanging in the sky.

Mountains are not only physical geographic landmarks, but also part of the very structure of the spirit world. The most part of the world delimiters of sacred landscape are mountains (Carmichael *et al.* 1997; Knapp and Ashmore 1999). For example, for the Western Apache in Arizona the physical and spiritual worlds intersect at several types of sites. The Most important of these are sacred mountains. Their importance relates mainly to their place in cosmology (Carmichael 1997: 92). Many mountains regarded as sacred in Japan, they are places which the gods inhabit (Higuchi 1989: 164-165). M. Eliade (1958: 99-100) argues that mountains are the nearest thing to the sky, and are thence endowed with a twofold holiness. They also share in the spatial symbolism of transcendence. They are the dwelling of deities, a spot where one can pass from one cosmic zone to another. Visual qualities of mountains make them the inevitable subjects of attention, despite the selective power of the eye. Symbolically important landscape features such as mountains may have generated myths. This mountain in the Island of Lesbos, possibly a symbolically important landscape feature, may have generated myths connected with the people living at Coşkuntepe.

Fig. VI.3. Uğurlu from the south

In the case of the island of Chios, the Ayio Gala Cave is possibly symbolically important. Ayio Gala means 'sacred milk' in Greek. This name was inspired by the continuous drip of water from an impressive stalactite in the upper cave (Hood 1981; 11). Caves are sacred places, associated with birth and regeneration (Carmichael *et al.* 1997). Caves are important sources of power; the kind of places where individuals can communicate directly with spirits. The entrance to the upper cave is behind the chapel of Panayia Galactonosera. In the upper cave, Archaic Greek and Roman pottery as well as Hellenistic and Roman figurines were recovered. Prehistoric material in the cave suggests that the cave was already in use as a sanctuary in the Neolithic period. The Early Neolithic material in the cave is related to finds from Western Anatolia. The cave was possibly symbolically important for the Western Anatolian Early Neolithic communities.

Such symbolically important places may have visited chiefly by men or shamans, seeking transcendence in order to achieve another level of jurisdiction over a domain more potent and supreme in its influence than that found in the everyday world.

The case of the island of Gökçeada is different. Gökçeada is about 17 km from the mainland. The whole island, possibly a symbolically important feature, may have generated myths connected with the Western Anatolian Neolithic communities. When we look at the island from the mainland and sail towards the island at different angles, different features and shapes may be seen. For Neolithic communities, Gökçeada may be a special place, characterized by different shapes and features (for example the Saami people see Bradley 2000: 6; the Wintu people see Theodoratus and LaPena 1997:23). Today topographical features of the islands still give meaning and distinction to the people. For example, the island of Bozcaada, close to Gökçeada, is known as the pregnant woman by the people living in the mainland. The fertility of women is reinforced by visiting it.

Fig. VI.4. Coşkuntepe and the view of the Island of Lesbos

65

I believe that a deep spiritual relation existed between the early communities and their natural surroundings. The islands having a given physical terrain have the power to cause human beings to form a particular type of mental images. Some of the islands might evoke images other than of a suitable place to live in. Nevertheless, people preferred to live because symbolic powers of the islands may have more important for them.

Conclusions

Early Neolithic settlements in the littoral region of Western Anatolia may have acted as base sites for Aegean navigators-fishers (Thissen 2000) and several such sites are linked to economic intensification with both the creation of a new domestic arena and the increased significance of a place-based world-view. I suggest that the subsistence of Western Anatolian littoral settlements was not totally dependent on domesticates. Thus, at least some of the Neolithic communities which moved to islands may not have been agriculturalists. Recent surveys in Western Anatolia have revealed new Early Neolithic sites, and a new Early Neolithic site was also found on the island of Gökçeada. The island of Gökçeada, compared which the other Eastern Aegean islands, is not a super-attractive island. There are a number of islands such as Lesbos and Samos with a much higher T/DR ranking than Gökçeada, but very late archaeological material. None of the colonization models indicate that Gökçeada is a more promising island for early colonization. So why Gökçeada? I suggest that the importance of islands may also lie in their symbolic significance. Landscapes provide locales foci in the symbolic construction of meaning. The meaning of landscapes becomes attached and unfolded in myths and rituals. Place-myths or ancestor-myths are closely related to place-images and these images are generally derived from visual experiences. The Neolithic people probably colonize those places where the symbolic construction of meaning had already established.

APPENDIX

14C DATES AT THE PREHISTORIC SETTLEMENTS OF EASTERN THRACE

Asagi Pinar

Lab. No.	Date BP	Material	Level	Cal BC 1 s.d	Cal BC 2 s.d
Bln-?	6781±39BP	?	6/7	5715-5635	5730-5620
Bln-?	6625±38BP	?	6	5620-5480	5630-5480
Bln-?	6374±48BP	?	5	5470-5300	5480-5260
Bln-?	6364±47BP	?	5	5470-5300	5480-5250
Bln-?	6341±43BP	?	5	5370-5260	5470-5210
Bln-?	6324±46BP	?	5	5370-5210	5470-5140
Bln-?	6282±45BP	?	5	5320-5140	5370-5070
Bln-?	6280±42BP	?	4/5	5320-5140	5340-5070
Bln-?	6322±34BP	?	4/5	5360-5210	5370-5150
Bln-?	6209±42BP	?	4	5260-5070	5300-5050
Bln-?	6267±48BP	?	4	5310-5080	5340-5060
Bln-?	6189±34BP	?	4	5230-5060	5280-5030
Bln-?	6260±40BP	?	4	5310-5140	5320-5070
Bln-?	6342±43BP	?	4	5370-5260	5470-5210
Bln-?	6054±41BP	Charcoal	4	5000-4850	5060-4800
Bln-?	6305±44BP	?	4	5340-5150	5380-5080
Bln-?	6107±51BP	?	4	5210-4860	5210-4850
Bln-?	6212±37BP	?	3	5260-5070	5300-5050
Bln-4608	6305±44BP	Charcoal	2	5340-5150	5380-5080
Bln-4607	6107±51BP	Charcoal	2	5210-4860	5210-4850

Hoca Çeşme

Lab. No.	Date BP	Material	Lavel	Cal BC 1 s.d.	Cal BC 2 s.d
Bln-4609	7637±43BP	?	IV	6500-6430	6590-6410
Hd-16725/119145	7496±69BP	?	IV	6420-6250	6460-6220
GrN-19779	7360±35BP	Charcoal	IV	6240-6100	6350-6080
GrN-19355	7200±180BP	Charcoal	IV	6230-5840	6400-5700
GrN-19357	7135±270BP	Charcoal	III	6230-5730	6500-5450
Hd-16724/17186	7239±29BP	?	III	6200-6020	6210-6010
Hd-16727/17038	7028±50BP	?	III	5990-5840	6010-5780
Hd-16726/17084	7005±33BP	?	III	5970-5810	5990-5790
GrN-19310	6890±280BP	Charcoal	II	6030-5520	6400-5300
GrN-19311	6960±65BP	Charcoal	II	5890-5740	5990-5720
GrN-19780	6920±90BP	Charcoal	II	5890-5710	5990-5640
GrN-19781	6900±110BP	Charcoal	II	5890-5660	6000-5610
GrN-19782	6890±60BP	Charcoal	II	5840-5710	5890-5640
GrN-19356	6520±110BP	Charcoal	II	5610-5360	5670-5290

Toptepe

Lab. No.	Date BP	Material	Level	Cal BC 1 s.d	Cal BC 2 s.d
HD-13590-13235	6095±40	Charcoal	5	5060-4860	5210-4840
HD-13589-13321	6155±40	Charcoal	5	5210-5000	5260-4950
GrN-18740	6160±70	?	5	5230-4990	5300-4850
GrN-18741	6200±50	?	5	5260-5060	5300-5000
GrN-16476	6290±25	Charcoal	5	5305-5210	5320-5140
HD-13591-13339	6410±180	?	4	5650-5050	5750-4850
GrN-18742	6060±110	?	3	5210-4800	5300-4700
GrN-18743	6220±70	?	3	5300-5060	5320-4950

Yarımburgaz Cave

Lab. No.	Date BP	Material	Level	Cal BC 1 s.d	Cal BC 2 s.d
GrN-15531	9190±100	Rottan plant?	7b	8530-8280	8690-8230
GrN-15533	7640±90	Charcoal	7a	6590-6400	6650-6250
GrN-15532	8180±320	Rottan plant ?	6	7500-6650	8000-6200
GrN-15529	7330±60	Charcoal	5 or 4a	6230-6080	6380-6020
GrN-18745	6650±280	?	4	5850-5300	6200-4900
GrN-15528	6880±90	Charcoal	3	5850-5660	5980-5620
GrN-18744	7130±90	?	2	6160-5890	6220-5800
GrN-15534	5930±110	Charcoal	2	4950-4620	5250-4500

14C data are calibrated with OxCal v3.5 using the recent calibration curve INTCAL98.

BIBLIOGRAPHY

Admiralty Handbook (1917) Turkey in Europe. London: War Staff Intelligence Division.

Admiralty Handbook (1942) Turkey I. London: War Staff Intelligence Division.

Akdeniz, E., 1997. 1995 yili Büyük Menderes Ovasi ve Çevresi Yüzey Araştirmalari. *XIV. Araştirma Sonuçlari Toplantisi II.* Ankara: 233-254.

Akman, M., 1997. Megalitforschung in Thrakien. *Istanbuler Mitteilungen* 47: 151-171.

Allen, M. J., 1991. Analysing the Landscape: a Geographical Approach to Archaeological Problems. In A. J. Schofield (ed.). *Interpreting Artefact Scatters. Contributions to Ploughzone Archaeology*: 39-57. Oxford: Oxbow Books.

Ammerman, A. J., 1985. Plow-zone experiments in Calabria, Italy. *Journal of Field Archaeology* 12: 33-40.

Angelov, N., 1959. Zlatnoto sykrovsce ot Hotnica. *Arkheologiya (Sofia)* 1/1-2:38-46.

Anthony, D. W., 1997. Prehistoric Migration as Social Process. In J. Chapman and H. Hamerow (eds), *Migrations and Invasions in Archaeological Explanation*: 21-32. International Series 664. Oxford: BAR.

Archibald, Z. H., 1998. *The Odrysian Kingdom of Thrace.* Oxford: Clarendon Press.

Arnuad, J. E. M., 1989. The Mesolithic Communities of the Sodo Valley, Portugal, in their Ecological Setting. In C. Bonsall (ed.), *The Mesolithic in Europe: Papers Presented at the 3th International Symposium*: 614-631. Edinburgh: Edinburgh University press.

Bailey, D. W., 1990. The living house: signifying continuity. In R. Samson (ed.), *The Social Archaeology of Houses*: 18-48. Edinburgh: Edinburgh University Press.

Bailey, D. W., 1997. Impermanence and Flux in the Landscape of Early Agricultural South Eastern Europe. In J. Chapman and P. Dolukhanov (eds), *Landscapes in Flux. Central and Eastern Europe in Antiquity*: 41-58. Oxford: Oxbow Books.

Bailey, D. W., 2000. *Balkan Prehistory. Exclusion, Incorporation and Identity.* London: Routledge.

Ballard, R.D., F.T. Hiebert, D.F. Coleman, C. Ward, J.S. Smith, K. Willes, B. Foley, K. Croff, C. Major and F. Torre. 2001. Deepwater Archaeology of the Black Sea: The 2000 Season at Sinop, Turkey. *American Journal of Archaeology* 105 / 4: 607-623.

Barrett, J., 1989. *Stone Circles of Britain.* British Series 215. Oxford: BAR.

Battaglia, D., 1983. Projecting personhood in Melanesia: the dialectics of artefact symbolism on Sabarl Island. *Man* 18: 289-304.

Battaglia, D., 1990. *On the Bones of the Serpent. Person, Memory and Mortality in Sabarl Island Society.* Chicago: University of Chicago Press.

Benac, A., 1973. *Obre II, a Neolithic Settlement of the Butmir Group at Gornje Polje.* Wissenschaftliche Mitteilungen des Bosnisch-Herzegowinischen Landesmuseums III :5-191. Sarajevo.

Berciu, D., 1966. *Culturâ Hamangia. Noi Contribuţii.* Bucharest: Institutul de Archeologia al Academiei RPR.

Binford, L. R. and S. R. Binford (eds). 1968. *New Perspectives in Archaeology.* Chicago: Aldine.

Binford, L. R., 1972. *An Archaeological Perspective.* New York: Seminar Press.

Binford, L. R., 1980. Willow smoke and dogs tails: hunter-gatherer settlement systems and archaeological site formation. *American Antiquity* 45:4-20.

Binford, L. R., 1983. Long-term land use patterns: some implications for archaeology. In R. Binford (ed.), *Working at Archaeology* : 379-386. New York: Academic press.

Bintliff, J. L., 1992. Appearance and Reality: Understanding the Buried Landscape Through New Techniques in Field Survey. In M. Bernardi (ed.). *Archeologia del Paesaggio*: 89-137. Firenze: All'Insegna del Giglio.

Bintliff, J. L., 1999. Settlement and Territory. In G. Barker (ed.), *Companion Encyclopedia of Archaeology.* Vol 1: 505-545. London and New York: Routledge.

Bintliff, J. L., 2000. The Concepts of "Site" and "Offsite" archaeology in the surface artefact survey. In M. Pasquinucci and F. Trement (eds.). *Non-Destructive Techniques Applied to Landscape Archaeology*: 200-215. The Archaeology of Mediterranean Landscapes 4. Oxford: Oxbow Books.

Bintliff, J. L. and A. M. Snodgrass. 1985. The Cambridge/Bradford Boeotian Expedition: The First Four Years. *Journal of Field Archaeology* 12: 123-161

Bintliff, J. L. and A. M. Snodgrass. 1988. Off-site Pottery Distributions: A Regional and Interregional Prespective. *Current Anthropology* 29/3: 506-510.

Bintliff, J. L., D. Oliver, P. Howard and A. Snodgrass. 2000. Deconstructing "The Sense of Place"? Settlemet Systems, Field Survey, and the Historic Record: a case-study from Central Greece. *Proceeding of Prehistoric Society* 66: 123-149.

Blackwood, B., 1950. *The Technology of a Modern Stone-Age People in New Guinea*. Oxford: Oxford University Press.

Borić, D., 1999. Places that created time in the Danube Gorges and beyond, c. 9000-5500 BC. *Documenta Praehistorica* XXVI: 41-70.

Borić, D., 2002. The Lepenski Vir conundrum: reinterpretation of the Mesolithic and Neolithic sequences in the Danube Gorges. *Antiquity* 76: 1026-1039.

Boyadziev, Y. D., 1995. Chronology of Prehistoric Cultures in Bulgaria. In D. W. Bailey and I. Panayatov (eds), *Prehistoric Bulgaria*. Monographs in World Archaeology 22 :149-191. Madison Wiskonsin: Prehistory press.

Bradley, R., 1998. *The Significance of Monuments: on the shaping of human experience in Neolithic and Bronze Age Europe*. London: Routledge.

Bradley, R., 2000. *An Archaeology of Natural Places*. London: Routledge.

Bradley, R., and M. Edmonds. 1993. *Interpreting the Axe Trade*. Cambridge: Cambridge University Press.

Broodbank, C., 1999. Colonization and Configuration in the Insular Neolithic of the Aegean. In P. Halstead (ed.), *Neolithic Society in Greece*: 15-41. Sheffield: Sheffield Academic Press.

Broodbank, C., 2000. *An Island Archaeology of the Early Cyclades*. Cambridge: Cambridge University Press.

Carmichael, D., 1997. Places of power: Mescalero Apache sacred sites and sensitive areas. In David Carmichael, Jane Hubert, Brian Reeves and Audhild Schanche (eds), *Sacred Sites, Sacred Places*: 89-98. London: Routledge.

Carmichael, D., J. Hubert, B. Reeves and A. Schanche (eds) 1997. *Sacred Sites, Sacred Places*. London: Routledge.

Černych, E. N., 1978. Ainbunar – a Balkan copper mine of the fourth millennium BC. *Proceedings of the Prehistoric Society* 44: 203-217.

Chapman, J., 1976. *The Balkans in the Fifth and Fourth Millennium BC*. Unpublished PhD thesis: University of London.

Chapman J., 1989. The Early Balkan Village. In S. Bökönyi (ed.), *Neolithic of Southeastern Europe and its Neareastern Connections*. Varia Archaeologica Hungarica II: 33-53. Budapest: Institute of Archaeology of Hungarian Academy of Science.

Chapman, J., 1990. Social inequality on Bulgarian tells and the Varna problem. In R. Samson (ed.), *The Social Archaeology of Houses*: 49-98. Edinburgh: Edinburgh University Press.

Chapman, J., 1991. The creation of social arenas in the Neolithic and Copper Age of South East Europe: the case of Varna. In P. Garwood, P. Jennings, R. Skeates and J. Toms (eds), *Sacred and Profane*: 152-171. Oxford: Oxbow Books.

Chapman, J., 1994. Social power in the early farming communities of Eastern Hungary-Perspectives from the Upper Tisza region. *Jósa András Múzeum Évkönyve* XXXVI : 79-99.

Chapman, J., 1998. Objectification, embodiment and the value of places and things. In D. Bailey (ed.). *The Archaeology of Value. Essays on prestige and the processes of valuation*: 106-130. Oxford: British Archaeological Reports (International Series 730).

Chapman, J., 2000a. *Fragmentation in archaeology. Persons, places and broken objects in the prehistory of South East Europe.* London: Routledge.

Chapman, J., 2000b. 'Rubbish-Dumps' or 'Places of Deposition'? Neolithic and Copper Age Settlements in Central and Eastern Europe. In A. Ritchie (ed.). *Neolithic Orkney in its European Context*: 347-362. Cambridge: McDonald Institute Monographs

Chapman, J., R. Shiel and Š. Batović. 1996. *The Changing face of Dalmatia: Archaeological and Ecological Studies in a Mediterranean Landscape.* Leicester: Leicester University Press.

Chappell, S., 1987. *Stone Axe Morphology and Distribution in Neolithic Britain.* British Series 177. Oxford: BAR.

Cherry, J. F. 1990. The first colonisation of the Mediterranean Islands: a review of recent research. *Journal of Mediterranean Archaeology* 3/2: 145-221.

Cherry, J. F., 1984. The initial colonization of the Western Mediterranean islands in the light of island biogeography and paleogeography. In W.H. Waldren, R. Chapman, J. Lewthwaite and R.-C. Kennard (eds.). *The Deya Conference of Prehistory: Early settlements in the Western Mediterranean islands and the Peripheral areas*: 7-23. International series 229. Oxford: BAR

Cherry, J. F., 1985. Islands out of stream: isolation and interaction in early east Mediterranean insular prehistory. In A.B. Knapp and T. Stech (eds.), *Prehistoric production and Exchange: The Aegean and Eastern Mediterranean*: 12-29. Los Angeles: UCLA Institute of Archaeology.

Cherry, J. F., J. L. Davis and E. Manzourani. 1991. *Landscape Archaeology as Long-Term History, Northern Keos in the Cycladic Islands.* Los Angeles: UCLA Institute of Archaeology.

Childe, V. G., 1929. *The Danube in Prehistory.* Oxford: Clarendon.

Childe, V. G., 1957 *The Dawn of European Civilisation.* 6th edition. London: Routledge and Kegan Paul Ltd.

Clark, H. R. and A. J. Schofield. 1991. By Experiment and Calibration: An Integrated Approach to Archaeology of Ploughsoil. In A. J. Schofield (ed.). *Interpreting Artefact Scatters. Contributions to Ploughzone Archaeology* : 93-105. Oxford: Oxbow Books.

Clark, J. G. D., 1965. Traffic in Stone Axe and Adze Blades. *Economic History Review* 18: 1-28.

Clark, J. G. D., 1989. *Economic Prehistory.* Cambridge: Cambridge University Press.

Clarke, D. L., 1968. *Analytical Archaeology.* London: Methuen.

Daniel, G. and C. Renfrew. 1988. *The Idea of Prehistory.* 2nd edition. Edinburgh: Edinburgh University press.

Davis, J. L., 1992. Review of Aegean Prehistory I: The Island of the Aegean. *American Journal of Archaeology* 96: 699-756.

Davis, S., 1989. Customary Sea Territories in Western Oceania. In J. Cordell (ed.), *A Sea of Small Boats*: 33-59. Cambridge, Massachusetts: Cultural Survival, Inc.

Degens, E.T and D.A. Ross (eds). 1974. The Black Sea-Geology, Chemistry and Biology. Menasha, Wisconsin: Collegiate Press.

Dennell, R. W and D. Webley. 1975. Prehistoric Settlement and Land use in Southern Bulgaria. In E. Higges (ed.), *Paleoeconomy*: 97-108. Cambridge: Cambridge University Press.

Deuser, W. G., 1972. Late-Pleistocene and Holocene History of the Black Sea as Indicated by Stable-Isotope Studies. *Journal of Geophysical Research* 77: 1071-1077.

Dewdney, J. C., 1971. *Turkey.* London: Chatto and Windus.

Dickson, F. P., 1981. *Australian Stone Hatchets. a study in design and dynamics.* Sydney: Academic Press.

Draganov, V., 1995. Submerged Coastal Settlements from the Final Eneolithic and Early Bronze Age in the Sea around Sozopol and the Urdoviza Bay near Kiten. In D.W. Bailey and I. Panayatov (eds), *Prehistoric Bulgaria*: 225-242. Madison: Prehistoric Press.

Dunnell, R. C. and W. S. Dancey. 1983. The siteless Survey: A Regional Scale Data Collection Strategy. *Archaeological Method and Theory* 6 : 267-287.

Edmonds, M., 1995. *Stone Tools and Society.* London: B.T. Batsford.

Eliade, M., 1958. *Patterns in Comparative Religion.* New York: New American Library.

Ercan, T., 1992. Trakya'daki Senozoyik Volkanizması ve Bölgesel Dağlımı. *Jeoloji Mühendisliği* 41: 37-50.

Erdoğu, B., 1997. Edirne ili 1995 Yılı Yüzey Araştırması. *XIV. Araştırma Sonuçları Toplantısı I*, Ankara: 273-291.

Erdoğu, B., 1999a. 1997 Yılı Edirne ili Yüzey Araştırması. *XVI. Araştırma Sonuçları Toplantısı II* , Ankara: 345-358.

Erdoğu, B., 1999b. The Late Chalcolithic Pottery from the Sites of Kavakli and Yumurta Tepe in the Province of Edirne, Eastern Thrace. *Proceedings of the Prehistoric Society* 65: 457-464.

Erdoğu, B., 2000. Problems of Dating Prehistoric Axe Factories and Neolithisation in Turkish Thrace. *Documenta Praehistorica* XXVII: 155-166.

Erdoğu, B., 2002. *The Neolithic and Chalcolithic Cultures in Turkish Thrace.* Unpublished PhD thesis: University of Durham.

Erdoğu, B., 2003a. Off-site Artefact Distribution and Land-use Intensity in Turkish Thrace. *Proceedings of the Prehistoric Society* 69: 183-200.

Erdoğu, B., 2003b. Visualizing Neolithic Landscape: The Early Settled Communities in Western Anatolia and Eastern Aegean Islands. *European Journal of Archaeology* 6(1): 7-23.

Erdoğu, B., O. Tanındı and D. Uygun. 2003. *Turkiye Arkeolojik Yerleşmeleri, 14C Veritabani.* Istanbul: Ege.

Erinç, S., 1954. The Pleistocene History of the Black Sea and Adjacent Countries with Special Reference to the Climatic Change. *Review of the Geographical Institute* I: 84-113.

Evans, J and T. O'Connor. 1999. *Environmental Archaeology. Principles and Methods.* Gloucester: Shire Sutton.

Fentress, J and C. Wickham. 1992. *Social Memory.* Oxford: Blackwell.

Flannery, K. V. (ed.) 1976. *The Early Mesoamerican Village.* London: Academic Press.

Foard, G., 1978. Systematic fieldwalking and the investigation of Saxon settlement in Northamptonshire. *World Archaeology* 9 / 3 : 357-374.

Fol, A.,R. Katinčarov, J. Lichardus, F. Bertemes and I. Karastev. 1989. Bericht über die bulgarisch-deutschen Ausgrabungen in Drama (1983-1988). *Bericht der Römisch-Germanischen Kommission* 70: 7-127.

Foley, R., 1977. Space and energy: a method for analysing habitat value and utilization in relation to archaeological sites: 163-187. In. D. L. Clarke (ed.). *Spatial Archaeology.* New York: Academic Press.

Foley, R., 1981a. *Off-site Archaeology and Human Adaptations in Eastern Africa.* International Series 97. Oxford: BAR.

Foley, R., 1981b. Off-site Archaeology: An Alternative Approach for the short-sighted. In I. Hodder, G. Issac and N. Hammond (eds.). *Pattern of the Past. Studies in Honour of David Clarke.* 157-183.Cambridge: Cambridge University Press.

French, D., 1964. Recent Archaeological reserch in Turkey, Surface Finds from Various Sites. *Anatolian Studies* 14: 35-37.

Gaffney, V. and M. Tingle. 1989. *The Maddle Farm Project.* British series 200. Oxford: BAR.

Gaffney, V., J. Bintliff and B. Slapšak. 1991. Site formation processes and Hvar Survey Project, Yugoslavia. In A. J. Scofield (eds.). *Interpreting Artefact Scatters: Contributions to Ploughzone Archaeology*: 59-80. Oxford:.Oxbow Books.

Georgieva, P., 1990, Periodization of the Krivodol-Salcuta-Bubanj Culture. In D. Srejović and N. Tasić (eds), *Vinča and its World*: *International Symposium The Danubian Region from 6000 to 3000 B.C.*: 169-173. Belgrade: Serbian Academy of Sciences and Arts Centre for Archaeological Research.

Gibson, J. J., 1979. *The Ecological Approach the Visual Perception.* Boston: Hougthon Mifflin.

Gimbutas, M. (ed.). 1976. *Neolithic Macedonia: as reflected by excavations at Anza.* Los Angeles:University of California, Institute of Archaeology.

Gimbutas, M., S. Winn and D. Shimabuku. 1989. *Achilleion: A Neolithic Settlement in Thessaly, Greece, 6400-5600 B.C.* Los Angeles: University of California, Institute of Archaeology.

Göçmen, K., 1976. *Asağı Meriç Vadisi Taşkın Ovası ve Deltanın Alüvyal Jeomorfolojisi.* Istanbul: IUCFY.

Gosden, C., 1989. Debt, Production and Prehistory. *Journal of Anthropological Archaeology* 8: 355-389.

Gould, R. A., 1968. Living Archaeology: the Ngatatjara of Western Australia. *Soutwestern Journal of Anthropology* 24: 101-122.

Greaves, M. A.. and B. Helwing. 2001. Archaeology in Turkey: The Stone, Bronze and Iron Ages, 1997-1999. *American Journal of Archaeology* 105: 463-511.

Gültekin, A. H., 1999. Şükrüpaşa sokulumu (Dereköy-Kırklareli) ile ilişkili Cu-Mo cevherlerinin jeolojik, mineralojik ve jeokimyasal özellikleri. *Türkiye Jeoloji Bülteni* 42/1: 29-45.

Gunterson C. G. and E. Özturgut. 1974. The Bosphorus. In E. T. Degens and D.A. Ross (eds), *The Black Sea - Geology, Chemistry and Biology*: 99-114. Menasha, Wisconsin: Collegiate Press.

Haddon, A. C., 1912. Science. In A. C Haddon (ed.), R*eports of Cambridge Anthropological Expedition to Torres Straits* 6: 218-237. Cambridge: Cambridge University press.

Halbwachs, M., 1980. *The Collective Memory.* London: Harper and Row.

Halstead, P., 1993. 'Spondylus' shell ornaments from the Late Neolithic Dimini, Greece: specialised manufacture or unequal accumulation? *Antiquity* 67: 603-609.

Hampton, O. W., 1999. *Culture of Stone. Sacred and Profane Uses of Stone Among the Dani.* Texas: Texas A&M University Press.

Harmankaya, S., O. Tanındı and M. Özbaşaran. 1997. *Türkiye Arkeolojik Yerlesmeleri II - Neolitik.* Istanbul:Ege.

Harmankaya, S. and B. Erdoğu. 2001. Prehistoric Survey at Gökçeada, Turkey, in 1999. *University of Durham and Newcastle Upon Tyne Archaeological Reports 1999/2000*: 28-35.

Harmankaya, S. and B. Erdoğu. 2002. *Türkiye Arkeolojik YerlesmeleriIVa-b – Ilk Tuc Caği. Istanbul:Ege.*

Harmankaya, S. and B. Erdoğu. 2003. Prehistoric sites at Gökçeada, Turkey. In M. Özdoğan, H. Hauptmann and N. Basgelen (eds), From Villages to Towns, Studies Presented to Ufuk Esin: 459-479. Istanbul: Arkeoloji ve Sanat.

Hayden, B. and A. Cannon. 1983. Where the Garbage Goes: Refuse Disposal in the Maya Highlands. *Journal of Anthropological Archaeology* 2: 117-163.

Hayes, P. P., 1991. Models for the distribution of pottery around former agricultural settlements. In A. J. Schofield (ed.) *Interpreting Artefact Scatters. Contributions to Ploughzone Archaeology*: 81-92. Oxford: Oxbow Books.

Higuchi, T., 1989. *The Visual and Spatial Structure of Landscapes.* Cambridge, Massachusetts: MIT press.

Hodder, I and C. Orton. 1976. *Spatial Analysis in Archaeology.* Cambridge: Cambridge University Press.

Hodder, I., 1982a. Towards a contextual approach to prehistoric exchange. In J. Ericson and T. Earle (eds), *Context for Prehistoric Exchange* : 199-211. New York: Academic Press.

Hodder, I., 1982b. *Symbols in Action.* Cambridge: Cambridge University Press.

Hodder, I., (ed.). 1982c. *Structural and Symbolic Archaeology.* Cambridge: Cambridge University Press.

Hood, S., 1981. *Excavations in Chios 1938-1955. Prehistoric Emporio and Ayio Gala.* London: The British School of Athens.

Huntley, B., 1990. European post-glacial forests: compositional changes in response to climatic change. *Journal of Vegetation Science* 1: 507-518.

Ivanov, I., 1989. Le necropole chalcolithique de Varna et les cités lacustres voisines. In *Le Premier Or de I'humanité en Bulgarie 5éme millénaire*: 30-33. Paris:Réunion des Musées nationaux.

Jacobs, K., 1995. Returning to Oleni' ostrov: Social, Economic and Skeletal Dimensions of a Boreal Forest Mesolithic Cemetery. *Journal of Anthropological Archaeology* 14: 359-403.

Jovanović, B., 1976. Rudna Glava - ein kupferbergwerk des frühen Eneolithikums in Ostserbien. *Der Anschnitt* 28: 150-157.

Keegan, W. F. and J. M. Diamond. 1987. Colonisation of islands by humans: a biogeographical perspective. In M. Schiffer (ed.), *Advances in Archaeological Method and Theory* 10: 49-92. New York: Academic Press.

Kelly, R. L., 1992. Mobility / Sedentism: Concepts, Archaeological Measures and Effects. *Annual Revue of Anthropology* 21 : 43-66.

Kent, S., 1989. Cross-Cultural perceptions of farmers as hunters and the value of meat. In S. Kent (ed.), *Farmers as Hunters: The Implication of Sedentism*: 2-17. Cambridge: Cambridge University Press.

Kerr, R. A., 1998. Black Sea Deluge May Have Helped Spread Farming. *Science* 279: 1132.

Kılıç, S., 2000. Marmara Bölgesi Ilk Tunç Cağı Yerleşmeleri. *1999 yılı Anadolu Medeniyetleri Muzesi Konferansları*: 29-44.

Klejn, L. S., 1982. *Archaeological Typology*. International series 153. Oxford: BAR.

Knapp, A. B. and W. Ashmore, 1999. Archaeological Landscapes: Constructed, Conceptualized, Ideational. In A. B. Knapp and W. Ashmore (eds), *Archaeologist of Landscape. Contemporary Prespectives*:1-30. Oxford: Blackwell.

Kristiansen K., 1984. Ideology and Material Culture: an Archaeological Perspective. In M. Spriggs (ed.), *Marxist Perspectives in Archaeology*: 72-100. Cambridge: Cambridge University Press.

Kurtoğlu, F., 1938. *Gelibolu Yöresi Tarihi*. Istanbul: Edirne ve Yöresi Eskieserleri sevenler kurumu yayinlari 3.

Lamb, H. H., 1982. Reconstruction of the course of post glacial climate over the world. In A. Harding (ed.), *Climatic Change in Later Pre-History*: 11-32. Edinburgh: Edinburgh University Press.

Lambeck, K., 1996. Sea-level change and shore-line evaluation in Aegean Greece since Upper Palaeolithic time. *Antiquity* 70: 588-611.

Leach, J. W. and E. Leach (eds). 1983. *The Kula. New Perspective on Massim Exchange*. Cambridge: Cambridge University Press.

Leshtakov, K. (ed.). 1997. *Maritsa Project I: Rescue Archaeological Excavations along Maritsa Motorway in South Bulgaria*. Sofia: Publication house "Roads Agency Ltd."

Lichardus, J., A. Fol, L. Getev, F. Bertemés, R. Echt, R. Katinčarov and I.K. Iliev. 2000. *Drama 1983-1999: Forschungen in der Mikroregion*. Bonn: Dr. Rudolf Habelt GMBH.

Macklin, M. G., J. Lewin and J. C. Woodward. 1995. Quaternary fluvial systems in the Mediterranean basin: 1-25. In J. Lewin, M.G. Macklin and J. C. Woodward (eds), *Mediterranean Quaternary River Environments*. Rotterdam: A.A. Balkama.

Magyari, E., B. Erdogu, R. Erdogu and J. Chapman. 2003. The Göl Baba pollen core: Contribution to the Holocene vegetation history of Turkish Thrace. *University of Durham and Newcastle Upon Tyne Archaeological reports 2001-2002*: 19-24.

Malinowski, B., 1922. *Argonauts of the Western Pacific*. London: Routledge.

Mansel, A. M., 1938. *Trakya'nin Kültür ve Tarihi*. Istanbul: Edirne ve Yöresi Eski Eserleri Sevenler Kurumu yay. 3.

Mantu, C-M., 1998. *Cultură Cucuteni. Evoluția Cronologia Legaturi*. Piatră-Neamţ: Muzeul de Istorie Piatra Neamt.

Mauss, M. G., 1925. *The Gift*. London: Routledge.

McArthur, R. H. and E. O. Wilson. 1967. *The Theory of Island Biogeography*. Princeton: Princeton University Press.

Meriç, E., 1995. *Quaternary Sequence in the Gulf of İzmit*: 349-351. İzmit: Harp Okulu Komutanligi Basim Evi.

MTA: http://www.mta.gov.tr/madenler/maden.asp

Murray, P., 1980. Discard Location: The Ethnographic Data. *American Antiquity* 45/3: 490-502.

Needham, S. P and T. Spence. 1997. Refuse and the formation of middens. *Antiquity* 71: 77-90.

Némeskeri, J. and I. Lengyel. 1976. Neolithic Skeletal Finds. In M. Gimbutas (ed.), *Neolithic Macedonia: as reflected by excavations at Anza*: 375-410. Los Angeles: University of California, Institute of Archaeology.

Neústupný, E., 1991. Community areas of prehistoric farmers in Bohemia. *Antiquity* 65: 326-331.

Neústupný, E., 1998. *Space in Prehistoric Bohemia*. Praha: Institute of Archaeology.

O'Shea, J and M. Zvelebil. 1984. Oleneostrovski mogilnik: Reconstructing the social and economic organization of Prehistoric Foragers in Northern Russia. *Journal of Anthropological Archaeology* 3: 1-40.

Ohnemus, S., 1998. *An Ethnology of the Admiralty Islanders*. Bathurst: Crawford House.

Özbek, O., 2000. A Prehistoric Stone Axe Production Site in Turkish Thrace: Hamaylitarla. *Documenta Praehistorica* XXVII: 167-171.

Özbek, O and K. Erol. 2001. Étude petrographique des haches polies du Hamylitarla et Fener-Karadutlar (Turquie). *Anatolia Antiqua* IX: 1-7.

Özdoğan, M., 1982. Tilkiburnu: a Late Chalcolithic Site in Eastern Thrace. *Anatolica* IX: 1-26.

Özdoğan, M., 1984. Doğu Marmara ve Trakya Araştırmaları 1982. *I. Araştırma Sonuçları Toplantısı*. Ankara: 63-68.

Özdoğan, M., 1985a. A Surface Survey for Prehistoric and Early Historic Sites in Northwestern Turkey. *National Geographic Research for 1979*: 517-541. Washington: National Geographic.

Özdoğan, M., 1985b. Marmara Bölgesinde Kültür Tarihi ile ilgili Bazi Sorunlar ve Bunlarin Çözümlenmesinde Jeomorfoloji Araştirmalarinin Katkisi. *Arkeometri Toplantisi Sonuçlari I*, Ankara: 39-62.

Özdoğan, M., 1986. Prehistoric Sites in the Gelibolu Peninsula. *Anadolu Araştirmalari* X: 51-66.

Özdoğan, M., 1988. 1986 yılı Trakya ve Marmara Bölgesi Araştırmaları. *V. Araştırma Sonuçları Toplantısı*. Ankara: 157-169.

Özdoğan, M., 1993. Vinča and Anatolia: a new look at a very old problem. *Anatolica* XIX:173-193.

Özdoğan, M., 1997. The Beginning of Neolithic Economies in Southeastern Europe: An Anatolian Prespective. *Journal of European Archaeology* 5/2 : 1-33.

Özdoğan, M., 1998a. Tarihöncesi Dönemlerde Anadolu ile Balkanlar Arasındaki Kültür Ilişkileri ve Trakya'da Yapılan Yeni Kazı Çalışmaları. *TÜBA-AR* 1: 63-93.

Özdoğan, M., 1998b. Hoca Çeşme: An Early Neolithic Anatolian Colony in the Balkans? In. P. Anreiter, L. Bartosiewicz, E. Jerem and W. Meid (eds), *Man and the Animal World. Studies in Archaezoology, Anthropology and Palaeolingustics in Memoriam Sandor Bökönyi*: 435-451. Budapest:Archaeolingua.

Özdoğan, M., 1999a. Anadolu'dan Avrupa'ya Açılan Kapı: Trakya. *Arkeoloji ve Sanat* 90: 2-28.

Özdoğan, M., 1999b. Northwestern Turkey: Neolithic Cultures in Between the Balkans and Anatolia. In M. Özdoğan and N. Başgelen (eds.), *Neolithic in Turkey. The cradle of civilization*: 203-224. Istanbul: Arkeoloji ve Sanat.

Özdoğan, M., (in press). The Black Sea, The Sea of Marmara and Bronze Age Archaeology. An Archaeological Predicament. *H. Todorova Festschrift*.

Özdoğan, M., Y. Miyake and N. Özbaşaran-Dede 1991. An Interim Report on the Excavations at Yarimburgaz and Toptepe in Eastern Thrace. *Anatolica* XVII : 59-121.

Özdoğan, M., H. Parzinger and N. Karul 1997. Kırklareli Kazılari (Aşağı Pınar and Kanlıgeçit Höyükleri). *Arkeoloji ve Sanat* 77: 2-11.

Özdoğan, M. and H. Parzinger 2000. Asagi Pinar and Kanligecit excavations- some new evidence an early metallurgy from eastern Thrace. U. Yalcin (ed.). *Anatolian Metal I*. Der Anschnitt, Beiheft 13: 83-91.

Parzinger, H. and M. Özdoğan. 1995. Die Ausgrabungen in Kirklareli (Turkisch-Thrakien) und ihre Bedeutung für die Kulturbeziehungen zwischen Anatolien und dem Balkan vom Neolithikum bis zur Frühbronzezeit. *Bericht der Römisch-Germanischen Kommission* 76: 5-29.

Patton, M., 1991. Axes, Man and Women: Symbolic Dimensions of Neolithic Exchange in Armorica (north-west France). In P. Garwood, P. Jennings, R. Skeates and J. Toms (eds), *Sacred and Profane*: 65-79. Oxford: Oxbow Books.

Patton, M., 1996. *Islands in Time: Island Sociogeography and Mediterranean Prehistory*. London: Routledge.

Perlès, C., 1992. Systems of exchange and organisation of production in Neolithic Greece. *Journal of Mediterranean Archaeology* 5: 115-164.

Perlès, C., 2001. *The Early Neolithic in Greece: the first farming communities in Europe*. Cambridge: Cambridge University Press.

Pernicka, E., F. Begemann, S. Schmitt-Strecker and G. A. Wagner. 1993. Eneolithic and Early Bronze Age Copper Artefacts from the Balkans and their Relation to Serbian Copper Ores. *Prähistorische Zeitscrift* 68 (1): 1-54.

Persons, E. C. 1919. Increase by Magic: A Zuni Pattern. *American Anthropologist* 21: 272-286.

Pétrequin, A.M. and P. Pétrequin. 1994. *Écologie d'un outil: la hache de pierre polie en Irian Jaya (Indonesie)*. Paris: CNRS.

Pétrequin, P., A. M. Pétrequin, F. Jeudy, C. Jeunesse, J. Monnier, J. Pélégrin and I. Praud. 1998. From the Raw Material to the Neolithic Stone Axe. Production Processes and Social Context. In M. Edmonds and C. Richards (eds), *Understanding the Neolithic of North-Western Europe*: 277-311. Glasgow: Cruithne Press.

Price, T. D., 1985. The Mesolithic of Western Europe. *Journal of World Prehistory* 1/3: 225-305.

Prinz B. 1988. The Ground Stone Industry from Divostin. In A. Mc Pherron and D. Srejović (eds), *Divostin and the Neolithic of Central Serbia*: 255-300. Pittsburgh: The Pittsburg University, Department of Anthropology.

Radovanović, I., 1996. *The Iron Gates Mesolithic*. Michigan: Prehistory Press.

Radunceva, C., 1989. La société dans les Balkans à l'age du cuivre. *Dossiers Histoire et Archéologie* 137: 46-55.

Relph, E., 1976. *Place and Placelessness*. London:Dion.

Renfrew, C., 1972. *The Emergence of Civilization*. London: Methuen.

Renfrew, C., 1986. Varna and the emergence of wealth in prehistoric Europe. In A. Appadurai (ed.), *The Social Life of Things*: 141-168. Cambridge: Cambridge University press.

Renfrew, C., J. Cann and J. Dixon. 1965. Obsidian in the Aegean. *Annual of the British School at Athens* 60: 225-247.

Rivière, P., 1995. House, places and People: community and continuity in Guiana. In J. Carsten and S. Hugh-Jones (eds.). *About the house: Lévi-Strauss and beyond*: 189-205. Cambridge: Cambridge University Press.

Robb, J., 2001. Island Identities: Ritual, Travel and the Creation of Difference in Neolithic Malta. *European Journal of Archaeology* 4 (2): 175-202.

Roche, J., 1989. Spatial Organisation in the Mesolithic sites of Muge, Portugal. In C. Bonsall (ed.), *The Mesolithic in Europe: Papers presented at the 3th International Symposium*: 607-613. Edinburgh: Edinburgh University Press.

Roper, D. C., 1976. Lateral displacement of artefacts due to plowing. *American Antiquity* 41:372-375.

Rowley-Conwy, P., 1998. Cemeteries, Seasonality and Complexity in the Ertebølle of Southern Scandinavia. In M. Zvelebil, R. Dennel and L. Domańska. *Harvesting the Sea, Farming the Forest. The Emergence of Neolithic Societies in the Baltic Region*: 193-202, Sheffield: Sheffield Academic Press.

Ryan W. B. F., W. C. Pitman, C. O. Major, K. Shimkus, V. Moskalenko, G. A. Jones, P. Dimitrov, N. Görür, M. Sakiç and H. Yüce. 1997. An abrupt drowning of the Black Sea shelf. *Marine Geology* 138: 119-126.

Ryan, W and W. Pitman. 1998. *Noah's Flood*. New York: Simon and Schuster.

Sahlins, M., 1972. *Stone Age Economics*. Chicago: Aldine.

Schama, S., 1995. *Landscape and Memory*. London: English Heritage.

Schulting, R., 1996. Antlers, bone points and flint blades: the Mesolithic cemeteries of Téviec and Hoëdic, Brittany. *Antiquity* 70: 335-350.

Seeher, J., 1990. Coşkuntepe- anatolisches Neolithikum am Nordostufer der Agais. *Istanbuler Mitteilungen* 40: 9-15.

Séfériadés, M., 2000. Spodylus Gaederopus: Some observations on the earliest European long distance exchange system. In S. Hiller and V. Nikolov (eds), *Karanovo III: Beiträge zum Neolithikum in Südosteuropa*:423-437. Wien: Phoibos Verlag.

Semenov, S. A., 1970. *Prehistoric Technology*. London: Cory, Adams and Mackay.

Shields, R., 1991. *Places on the Margin. Alternative Geographies of Modernity*. London: Routledge.

Shilik, K. K., 1997. Oscillations of the Black Sea and Ancient Landscapes. In. J. Chapman and P. Dolukhanov (eds), Landscapes in Flux. Central and Eastern Europe in Antiquity. Oxford: Oxbow Books.

Stanley, D. J. and C. Blanpied. 1980. Late Quaternary Water Exchange Between the Eastern Mediterranean and the Black Sea. *Nature* 285: 537-541.

Strathern, M., 1988. *The Gender of the Gift: Problems with women and problems with society in Melanesia*. Berkeley: University of California Press.

Taçon P., 1991. The power of stone: symbolic aspects of stone use and tool development in western Arnhem Land, Australia. *Antiquity* 65: 192-207.

Taylor, J., 2000. Cultural depositional processes and post-depositional problems. In R. Francovich, H. Patterson and G. Barker (eds.). *Extracting meaning from ploughsoil assemblages*: 16-26. The Archaeology of Mediterranean Landscapes V. Oxford: Oxbow Books.

Tegart, W. J. M., G. W. Sheldon and D. C. Graffits. 1990. *Climate Change*. The IPCC impacts assessment. Canberra: Australian Government Publishing Service.

Ternek, Z., 1987. *Explanatory Text of the Geological Map of Turkey: Istanbul*. Ankara: MTA.

Theodoratus, J. D. and F. LaPena. 1997. Wintu sacred geography of Northern California. In David Carmichael, Jane Hubert, Brian Reeves and Audhild Schanche (eds), *Sacred Sites, Sacred Places*: 20-31. London: Routledge.

Thissen, L., 1999. Trajectories towards the neolithisation of NW Turkey. *Documenta Praehistorica* XXVI: 29-39.

Thissen, L., 2000. Thessaly, Franchthi and Western Turkey: Clues to the Neolithisation of Greece? *Documenta Praehistorica* 27: 141-154.

Thissen, L., 2002. Appandix I: CANeW C14 databases and C14 charts, Anatolia, 10.000-5000 cal BC. In F. Gérard and L. Thissen (eds), *The Neolithic of Central Anatolia*: 299-337. Istanbul: Ege.

Thomas J. and C. Tilley. 1993. The Axe and the Torso: Symbolic Structures in Neolithic of Brittany. In C. Tilley (ed.), *Interpretative Archaeology*: 225-324. Oxford: Berg.

Thomas, D. H., 1975. Non-site sampling in Archaeology: Up the Creek without site? In J. W. Muller (ed.) *Sampling in Archaeology* : 61-81. Tuscon: University of Arizona press.

Tilley, C., 1994. *A Phenomenology of Landscape. Place, Paths and Monuments*. Oxford: Berg.

Tilley, C., 1996. *An Ethnography of the Neolithic: Early Prehistoric Societies in Southern Scandinavia*. Cambridge: Cambridge University Press.

Tilley, C., 1999. *Metaphor and Material Culture*. Oxford: Blackwell.

Todorova, H., 1978. *The Eneolithic in Bulgaria*. International Ser.49. Oxford: BAR.

Todorova, H., 1986, *Kamennomednata epocha v Bulgarija*. Sofia: Nauka i Izkustuo.

Todorova, H., 1989. Le période chalcolithique en Bulgarie: une civilisation préurbaine. In *Le Premier Or de I'humanité en Bulgarie 5éme millénaire*: 30-33. Paris: Réunion des Musées nationaux.

Todorova, H., 1993. Die Protobronzezeit auf der Balkanhalbinsel. *Anatolica* XIX: 307-318.

Todorova, H., 1995. The Neolithic, Eneolithic and Transitional Period in Bulgarian Prehistory. In D. W. Bailey and I. Panayatov (eds), *Prehistoric Bulgaria*. Monographs in World Archaeology 22: 79-98. Madison Wiskonsin: Prehistory press.

Torrence, R., 1986. *Production and Exchange of Stone Tools*. Cambridge: Cambridge University Press.

Tuan, Yi-Fu. 1977. *Space and Place. The Perspective of Experience*. London: Arnold.

van Andel, T. H. and C. N. Runnels. 1995. The Earliest Farmers in Europe. *Antiquity* 69: 481-500.

van Andel, T. H., 1989. Late Quaternary sea-level changes and archaeology. *Antiquity* 63: 733-745.

van Andel, T. H., K. Gallis and G. Toufexis. 1995. Early Neolithic farming in a Thessalian river landscape. In L. Lewin, M. G. Macklin and J. C. Woodward (eds), *Mediterranean Quaternary River Environments*: 131-144. Rotterdam: Balkema.

Vita-Finzi, C. and E. S. Higgs. 1970. Prehistoric economy in the Mount Carmel area of Palestine: site catchment analysis. *Proceedings of the Prehistoric Society* 36: 1-37.

Voytek, B., 1990. The use of stone resources. In R. Tringham and D. Krstić (eds), *Selevec: A Neolithic Village in Yugoslavia*. Los Angeles: University of California Press.

Wagner, A.G. and Ö. Özturnali 2000. Prehistoric Copper in Turkey. U. Yalcin (ed.) *Anatolian Metal I*. Der Anschnitt, Beiheft 13: 31-67.

Wagner, R., 1975. *The Invention of Culture*. Englewood Cliffs, NJ: Prenticen-Hall Inc.

White J.P. and N. Modjeska. 1978. Where do all the stone tools go? Some examples and problems in their social and spatial distribution in the Papua New Guinea Highlands. In I. Hodder (ed.), *Spatial Organisation of Culture* : 25-38. London: Duckworth.

Whittle, A., 1996. *Europe in the Neolithic: The Creation of New Words*. Cambridge: Cambridge University Press.

Whittle, A., 1997. Moving on and Moving around: Neolithic settlement mobility. In P. Topping (ed.), *Neolithic Landscapes*: 15-22. Oxford: Oxbow books.

Whittle, A., 2001. From mobility to sedentism: change by degrees. In R. Kertész and J. Makkay (eds.). *From the Mesolithic to the Neolithic*: 447-461. Budapest: Archaeolingua.

Wilkie, N. C and M. C. Savina. 1997. The earliest farmers in Macedonia. *Antiquity* 71: 201-207.

Wilkinson, T. J., 1982. The Definition of Ancient Manured Zones by Means of Extensive Sherd-Sampling Techniques. *Journal of Field Archaeology* 9: 323-333.

Wilkinson, T. J., 1989. Extensive Sherd Scatters and Land-use Intensity: Some Recent Results. *Journal of Field Archaeology* 16: 31-46.

Williams, N., 1982. A boundarie is to cross: observations on Yolngu boundaries and permission. In N. Williams and E. Hunn (eds), Resource Managers: North-American and Australian Hunter-Gatherers. Boulder, Colorado: Westview Press.

Wright, J. C., J .F. Cherry, J. L. Davis, E. Mantzourani and S. B. Sutton. 1990. The Nemea Valley Archaeological Project a Preliminary Report. *Hesperia* 59 / 4: 579-645.

Yellen, J., 1977. *Archaeological Approaches in the present: Models for Reconstructing the Past*. New York: Academic Press.

Yordanov, D., 1938-39. Rastitelnite Otnoshenia v Bulgarskite Chasti na Strandja Planina. *Annuare del'Universite de Sofia. II Faculte de Physic et Mathematique* XXXV/3: 1-90.

Zbenovich, G. V., 1996. The Tripolye Culture: Centenary of Research. *Journal of World Prehistory* 10/2:199-237.

Zvelebil, M., 1998. What's in a name: the Mesolithic, the Neolithic and social change at the Mesolithic-Neolithic transition. In M. Edmonds and C. Richards (eds), *Understanding the Neolithic of Northwestern Europe*: 1-3. Glasgow: Cruithne Press.